AN INTRODUCTION TO KARL MARX

# An Introduction to Karl Marx

*JON ELSTER*

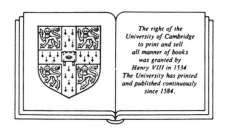

The right of the
University of Cambridge
to print and sell
all manner of books
was granted by
Henry VIII in 1534
The University has printed
and published continuously
since 1584.

CAMBRIDGE UNIVERSITY PRESS

*Cambridge*

*New York   New Rochelle   Melbourne   Sydney*

Published by the Press Syndicate of the University of Cambridge
The Pitt Building, Trumpington Street, Cambridge CB2 1RP
32 East 57th Street, New York, NY 10022, USA
10 Stamford Road, Oakleigh, Melbourne 3166, Australia

First published 1986
Reprinted 1987, 1988

Printed in the United States of America

*Library of Congress Cataloging-in-Publication Data*
Elster, Jon, 1940–
An introduction to Karl Marx.
Includes bibliographies.
1. Marx, Karl, 1818–1883.   I. Title.
HX39.5.E43   1986      335.4       86–4238
ISBN 0 521 32922 1 hard covers
ISBN 0 521 33831 X paperback

# CONTENTS

# Contents

# PREFACE

In 1985 I published a lengthy book on Marx, *Making Sense of Marx* (Cambridge University Press). The present book is much shorter, about 25 percent of the first. It has virtually no exegetical discussions of the texts or of the views of other Marxist scholars. The main intention is simply to state Marx's views and engage in an argument with them. With two exceptions, there is little here that is not found, in some place and some form, in the first book. In Chapter 1, I provide a brief bio-bibliographic survey that is not included in *Making Sense of Marx*. In Chapter 3, I offer a discussion of alienation that goes substantially beyond what was found in the earlier book. A fuller development of the ideas sketched there is found in my "Self-realization in work and politics," *Social Philosophy and Policy* (1986).

A companion volume of selected texts by Marx, organized along thematic lines corresponding to Chapters 2–9, is published simultaneously with this book.

# 1

# OVERVIEW

ONE hundred years after his death, Marx is an enormous presence among us. On purely quantitative criteria, judged by the number of his self-avowed followers, he exerts a greater influence than any of the religious founders or any other political figures. His doctrine being secular rather than timeless, we would not expect it to have the staying power of Islam, Christianity, or Buddhism, but up to now it has shown few signs of waning. It is not difficult to justify a continued interest in his writings.

The interest may be extrinsic or intrinsic. One may go to Marx to understand the regimes that have been influenced by him, or to understand and assess his writings as if he had had no posterity whatever. Of these, the former requires the latter, but not the other way around. When a doctrine – be it religious or political – becomes an institutional force, it always becomes the object of intense scrutiny in its own right, because the proper interpretation may be a matter of momentous importance. This is not to say that all dogmatic controversies are decided on purely internal criteria of validity or consistency. Many of them owe their resolution to mundane struggles of power, in which, however, purely textual arguments serve as one form of ammunition. Although textual considerations and rational assessment by themselves probably do not set constraints on the outcome, they may in some cases tip the balance one way or the other. The student of political processes in contemporary communist societies will do well, therefore, to know the texts that form part of the arsenal of debate. Although Engels and Lenin are the more frequently cited, Marx provides the final touchstone.

The guiding interest in the present exposition is, however, purely intrinsic. This will be taken to mean three things. First, it is a matter of establishing *what Marx thought*. This task is subject to the usual principles of textual analysis: to understand each part in the light of the whole and when in doubt to choose the reading that makes the texts appear as plausible and as consistent as possible. In Marx's case the task presents unusual difficulties. For one thing, the bulk of the corpus consists of unpublished manuscripts and letters in a very uneven state of completion. Some of them, though preserved for posterity, are still unpublished, so that no interpretation can claim to be based on all surviving texts. For another, the published writings are largely journalistic or agitatorial and as such are unreliable guides to his considered opinion. There is, moreover, the problem of ascertaining what was written by Marx and what by Engels and whether the latter's writings can be used as evidence for Marx's views. Finally, one must take account of the fact that Marx's thought changed over time, including both discontinuous breaks and more gradual evolution.

We have, in fact, only two published writings that show us Marx at the height of his theoretical powers: *The Eighteenth Brumaire of Louis Bonaparte* and the first volume of *Capital*. They make up approximately one thousand pages, of a corpus of perhaps thirty thousand. They form, as it were, the fixed point from which the other writings may be surveyed and guide the choice between different readings. They do not suffice, however, to eliminate all ambiguities – among other things because they are far from perfectly clear and consistent themselves. Even in his most carefully written works, Marx's intellectual energy was not matched by a comparable level of intellectual discipline. His intellectual profile is a complex blend of relentless search for truth, wishful thinking, and polemical intent. Between the reality he observed and his writings, there intervened at least two distorting prisms, first in the formation of his thought and then in the way he chose to express it.

The operation of the first kind of bias is most evident in his views on communist society – whether communism as he conceived it was at all possible, and whether it would come about in the course of history. He seems to have proceeded on two implicit assumptions: First, whatever is desirable is feasible; second, whatever is desirable and feasible is inevitable. The second kind of bias is most clearly seen in his political writings. There is the bias of compromise, due to the need to reconcile different factions; the bias of exhortation, arising from the desire to use "the analysis of the situation" as a means to changing it; and the bias of anticipated censorship, which operated when he had to disguise or tone down his views to be allowed to state them at all.

Next, I shall ask *whether Marx was right* in what he thought on the numerous issues – historical as well as theoretical – that he confronted. This examination will involve deliberate anachronism, in the sense that it will draw on facts and theories not available to Marx. In particular, the exposition of Marx's economic theories will use language developed much after his death. I shall also have the occasion to point out that on various factual matters Marx has been proved wrong by more recent scholarship. In fact, by and large it will appear that strictly speaking Marx was almost never "right." His facts were defective by the standards of modern scholarship, his generalizations reckless and sweeping.

A more interesting question, however, is *whether Marx remains useful* for us today. Which of Marx's theories are hopelessly dated or dead, and which remain a source of new ideas and hypotheses? To answer this question we must look at the wood, not just at the trees. As in the somewhat similar case of Freud, we may find that a theory can be shot through with errors of detail, even have basic conceptual flaws, yet remain immensely fertile in its overall conception. It is in the nature of the case that such assessments must be somewhat vague. The Marxian ancestry of a given line of inquiry may not be obvious and is certainly not proven by the claim of its practitioners to be among his descendants. Yet there exist unmistakably Marxian theories of alienation, exploitation, technical change, class struggle, and ideology that remain viable and vital.

The organizing idea of the exposition, therefore, is to set out what I believe were Marx's views on the central issues before him, to assess their validity in the light of the best knowledge available to us today, and to discuss whether the general conceptions underlying them can be useful even when his specific implementation is flawed. The range of issues covers normative as well as explanatory problems. I take the view that Marxism includes both a specific conception of the good life and a specific notion of distributive justice, in addition to a theory of history and an analysis of capitalism. The emphasis on normative issues is probably the most distinctive and controversial feature of the exposition. Most other commentators affirm that Marx denied the existence of absolute values, some of them seeing in this a cause for praise and others for blame.

Can one be a Marxist today? The overriding goal of the exposition is to help the reader form an answer to this question. Many would say, both on intellectual and on moral grounds, that it is no longer possible to be a "Marxist." Many of Marx's most cherished doctrines have been totally demolished by argument. Others have been refuted by history, which has shown us that the logical consequence of his political philosophy is an abhorrent social system. What little remains can be and largely has been absorbed into mainstream social thought.

Each of these three arguments may be countered. To the question whether I am a Marxist, or why, on intellectual grounds, I would want to call myself a Marxist, I have a well-rehearsed answer: "If, by a Marxist, you mean someone who holds all the beliefs that Marx himself thought were his most important ideas, including scientific socialism, the labor theory of value, the theory of the falling rate of profit, the unity of theory and practice in revolutionary struggle, and the utopian vision of a transparent communist society unconstrained by scarcity, then I am certainly not a Marxist. But if, by a Marxist, you mean someone who can trace the ancestry of his most important beliefs back to Marx, then I am indeed a Marxist. For me this includes, notably, the dialectical method and the theory of alienation, exploitation, and class struggle, in a suitably revised and generalized form."

Among intellectuals in Eastern Europe, with few exceptions, "Marxism" is a dirty word. To them it signifies not the liberation but the oppression of man. The view is encapsulated in Solzhenitsyn's refusal to meet Sartre in Moscow and memorably argued in Kolakowski's *Main Currents of Marxism*. It is an attitude that commands great respect, but its implications for the understanding of Marx are somewhat unclear. True, the work of Marx was one of

4

the causes that led to the Soviet regime; equally true, that regime justifies itself through Marx, asserting that it is roughly the kind of regime he wanted to bring about. That assertion is manifestly false. Yet the real question lies elsewhere. It is whether any attempt to bring about the kind of regime he wanted necessarily has to employ means that will in fact bring about something roughly similar to the Soviet regime. This I deny. Yet I shall also argue that an attempt to achieve the goal by means of a violent proletarian revolution will be self-defeating. The revolutionary bid for power can succeed only under conditions of backwardness that will also prevent, not only initially but indefinitely, the flowering of the productive forces that Marx posed as a condition for communism as he understood it.

It would seem, finally, that Marxism as a body of positive social theory, concerned with establishing and explaining facts, ought to disappear if it is bad and also if it is any good. In the latter case its findings will enter the main body of the historical and social sciences and cease to be specifically "Marxist." The identity and survival of Marxism is linked, however, to its normative foundation. Because of their adherence to specific, not universally shared values, Marxist scholars ask different questions. In arguing for their answers, on the other hand, they have to follow the same canons of method and reasoning as other scholars. Because of their values they look for different things to explain, but the logic of explanation is the same. Their theories will, if plausible, enter the mainstream of social science if they can also be useful to scholars who ask other questions; and if they cannot it is a good bet that they are not very plausible.

## MARX: LIFE AND WRITINGS

Because of the great variety and diversity of Marx's writings, it is often useful to know when, under which circumstances, for which purposes, and for which public they were written. The following chronological survey of his writings is meant to facilitate the more systematic discussions in later chapters. It is *not* intended as a biographical sketch. Only information about Marx's life directly relevant to the understanding of his work is included.

*1818–1835: Trier.* Marx grew up in the town of Trier in Prussian Rhineland, a formerly liberal province now under a harshly oppressive regime. Both his parents descended from rabbinical families, but his father converted the whole family to Protestantism to escape discrimination against Jews. Much has been made of Marx's Jewish background and the alleged self-hatred that led him to espouse anti-Semitism. There is something to the allegation, but Marx's anti-Semitism never took a virulent practical form. His attitude toward the Slavonic peoples – his "Russophobia" – was in fact more deeply shaped by racism.

*1835–1841: University studies.* Upon leaving school, Marx studied briefly at the University of Bonn and then for five years in Berlin. Here he came to know the philosophy of Hegel and met a group of left-wing philosophers known as the "Young Hegelians," who were mainly concerned with the critique of religion. He wrote his doctoral dissertation on "The Difference between the Philosophies of Nature in Democritus and Epicurus," an echo of which is found in the frequent references in later works to the trading nations who live "in the pores of society, like the Gods of Epicurus." The Hegelian imprint these years gave to his thinking never wore off completely, although it is not equally apparent in all his writings.

*1842–1843: Journalism and philosophy.* During this period Marx worked as journalist and then as editor for the Cologne newspaper *Rheinische Zeitung.* His articles show him to be a radical liberal, concerned with freedom of the press and protection of the poor, without, however, seeing the latter as the agent of their own emancipation. After the paper was suppressed by the government in early 1843, Marx devoted a long summer to philosophical studies. One fruit of this activity is *The Critique of Hegel's Philosophy of Right,* a commentary on §§261–313 of Hegel's work. The work was first published in this century. Another, the essay "On the Jewish Question," shows Marx from his worst side as a writer. It is replete with overblown and obscure rhetoric as well as offending remarks about Judaism. It remains of some interest, however, because it contains Marx's only statement on the rights of man, which he characterizes as "the rights of egoistic man, of man separated from other men and from the community."

*1843–1845: Paris and communism.* From late 1843 to early 1845

Marx lived in Paris. He became a communist and in the article "Critique of Hegel's Philosophy of Right: Introduction" stated his belief that the proletariat must emancipate itself and thereby the whole of society. He also wrote a long critique of capitalism, variously known as *The Paris Manuscripts* or *Economic and Philosophical Manuscripts of 1844*, published only in this century. The notion of the alienation of man under capitalism is the central theme. In Paris he also began his lifelong friendship with Friedrich Engels and collaborated with him on an exuberantly juvenile refutation of the Young Hegelians, *The Holy Family; or, Critique of Critical Criticism.*

*1845–1848: Brussels.* Marx had been active among the émigré German politicians in Paris and, as a result of pressure from the Prussian government, had to leave Paris for Brussels. He remained active in politics, first on a local and then on a European scale. Three important writings punctuate these years. In 1845–6 he and Engels collaborated on the posthumously published *German Ideology*, in which historical materialism emerged in full-fledged form, or at least as fully fledged as it ever came to be. In 1847 he published *Misère de la Philosophie*, a reply to P.-J. Proudhon's *Philosophie de la Misère*, which had appeared the previous year. In the heavily ironic style he had not yet discarded, Marx makes fun of Proudhon's attempt to master the Hegelian dialectic and of his petty-bourgeois outlook. In 1848 Marx and Engels collaborated on *The Communist Manifesto*, published in London by the Communist League. This masterpiece of political propaganda contains a sweeping historical overview and extravagant praise of the civilizing power of capitalism, concluding that "what the bourgeoisie produces, above all, is its own gravediggers." By this time two of the three major pieces of Marx's doctrine were in place: the theory of alienation and historical materialism. The theory of exploitation existed in an embryonic stage but was not fully worked out until many years later.

*1848–1849: Revolution in Germany.* On 26 February 1848 news of the revolution in Paris reached Brussels. A week later Marx arrived in Paris and left for Cologne in early April to become editor of the *Neue Rheinische Zeitung*, which published 300 issues before it folded in May 1849. In its pages Marx initially encouraged the

German bourgeoisie to pursue the work of the democratic revolution, but when they shied away from what in his view was their historical mission, his policy took a leftward turn. He could not, however, stem the counterrevolutionary tide. When he was expelled from Germany in May 1849, he also left active politics for fifteen years, not counting émigré squabbles in London.

*1850–1852: The sociology of French politics.* From August 1849 to his death Marx lived in London, interrupted by a few brief visits abroad. In the short-lived *Neue Rheinische Zeitung: Politisch-ökonomische Revue,* he wrote a series of articles on French politics, which were published by Engels in 1895 as *The Class Struggles in France.* They cover the period from the outbreak of the February Revolution to August 1850. *The Eighteenth Brumaire of Louis Bonaparte* was published in 1852 and covers the whole period from 1848 to Louis Napoleon's coup d'état in December 1851. These writings remain our main source for the understanding of Marx's theory of the capitalist state, together with the contemporary articles on English politics.

*1850–1878: Economic studies and writings.* In June 1850 Marx obtained a ticket to the Reading Room in the British Museum, thus beginning the economic studies that eventually led to the three volumes of *Capital.* The road was long, twisted, and thorny. Of the numerous manuscripts Marx produced in these years, only two – *Critique of Political Economy* and *Capital I* – were published in his lifetime. The publication of the others has been scattered over a century, from 1884 to 1982. To help the reader orient himself in this wilderness, I shall indicate the date of writing and of publication of these manuscripts, as well as their relation to one another.

*1857–1858: Grundrisse der Kritik der politischen Ökonomie.* This huge manuscript – 1,000 printed pages – was first published in Moscow in 1939–41 but was not available to Western scholars until the East German publication in 1953. It is partly an impenetrable Hegelian thicket, partly a wonderfully inspiring study of economic philosophy and economic history. It is perhaps the freshest and most engaging of all Marx's works, one in which his ideas can be studied *in statu nascendi.*

*1859: A Critique of Political Economy.* This work corresponds to the first and least interesting part of the *Grundrisse.* Its place in the history of Marxism is due to the important preface where Marx summarized, in a single long paragraph, the basic tenets of historical materialism. Until the publication in 1926 of the first part of *The German Ideology*, these few sentences remained the only authoritative statement of the theory.

*1861–1863: Zur Kritik der politischen Ökonomie.* This enormous manuscript – 2,300 printed pages – consists of twenty-one notebooks. Of these, notebooks 6 through 15 were published by Karl Kautsky in 1906–8 as *Theories of Surplus-Value.* They deal mainly with the history of economic thought, but contain also important substantive passages. The remaining notebooks were published in 1976–82, in the new scholarly edition of Marx's and Engels's collected works (see the section, "Editions of Marx's Writings"). They are preliminary studies to the first and third volumes of *Capital,* and supplement them on some points.

*1865: Results of the Immediate Process of Production.* This manuscript was published in Moscow in 1933 but was first made available to Western scholars in 1969. It was intended to serve as a bridge between the first and the second volumes of *Capital.*

*1867: Capital I.* This book is beyond doubt and comparison Marx's most important work. It stands with Darwin's *Origin of Species* as the most influential book of the nineteenth century. Although Marx intended it to serve the cause of the working class, it is also and preeminently a book for the happy few, by one of them. Marx assumes that *his* readers know Greek, Latin, and the major European languages; that they are capable of recognizing remote allusions to literary and philosophical works, besides being thoroughly familiar with arcane matters of political economy. It is carried by a white-burning indignation that is all the more effective for being more disciplined than in Marx's earlier works, which were often marred by heavy sarcasm. Considered as economic analysis it was not a lasting achievement, but it remains unsurpassed as a study of technical change, entrepreneurial behavior, and class conflict in the age of classical capitalism.

*1865–1878: Capital II.* This work, published by Engels in 1884, is with a few exceptions utterly boring and, unlike the two other volumes, does not repay reading for anyone but Marx scholars. Marx's attempt to draw interesting conclusions from simple accounting principles was not successful. The exceptions are the schemes of simple and extended reproduction, which anticipate modern input–output analysis, although the gist of Marx's analysis can be stated in one page whereas he uses more than one hundred.

*1864–1875: Capital III.* This work, published by Engels in 1894, is much more valuable. The chapters on economic history are among Marx's most important writings. The chapters on value theory and crisis theory contain his most authoritative statements on these topics. It must be added, however, that the scholarly consensus today is that these theories are seriously, perhaps irreparably, flawed. The nonspecialist reader will not profit much from struggling with Marx's exposition of them.

*1852–1862: American journalism.* To earn a living, Marx wrote about five hundred articles, over a period of ten years, as European correspondent for the *New York Daily Tribune,* a leading American newspaper of progressive persuasions. Many of his contributions are small masterpieces of historical and political analysis, notably the articles on the British rule in India and the numerous articles on English politics, which form a useful supplement to the writings on France. In others one is more struck by his bias than his acumen, as when he touches upon one of his *bêtes noires,* the British foreign minister Lord Palmerston or Napoleon III.

*1864–1872: The First International.* Marx played a leading, in fact dominating, role in the International Working Men's Association, an organization of European trade unions. Marx penned the inaugural address and the provisional rules of the International and was elected to the General Council, which was in charge of day-to-day affairs between the annual congresses. Its first years were marked by Marx's successful struggle against one anarchist faction, the followers of Proudhon; the last years by the unsuccessful struggle against another, grouped around Mikhail Bakunin. The most important written work from this period is *The Civil War in France,* a postmortem on the revolutionary insurrection in 1871 known as the Paris Commune.

*1873–1883: Last years.* The last years of Marx's life were marked by ill health. He worked on the manuscripts for *Capital* but without much progress. He guided from a distance the emerging working-class movement in Germany and wrote an important commentary – *The Critique of the Gotha Program* – on a document that was drawn up when the two socialist parties in Germany merged in 1875. He took an interest in Russian history and society and corresponded with Russian socialists about the proper strategy for revolution in a backward country not yet permeated by capitalism.

### MARX AND ENGELS

Friedrich Engels (1820–95) collaborated closely with Marx over a period of forty years. In the eyes of posterity, especially in the communist countries, they have merged into one entity, Marx-and-Engels. Even scholars sometimes assume without much argument that statements by Engels can be used to support this or that interpretation of Marx. The present exposition is guided by the opposite principle: Only statements by Marx are used to argue that Marx held this or that view.

Marx was a genius, a force of nature. Engels was a minor, prolific, somewhat pedantic writer. He began the tradition of codifying Marx's thought into a total system that promises answers to all questions in philosophy, the natural sciences, and the social sciences. The polemical work *Anti-Dühring*, in particular, became immensely influential, especially the discussion of dialectics. It is a fact of major tragicomical proportions that a third of mankind professes these naive, amateurish speculations as its official philosophy. It is often argued that because Marx read the manuscript to *Anti-Dühring*, and as far as we know did not object to it, its views can be imputed to him en bloc. The argument is worthless. Marx was constitutionally incapable of arriving at his conclusions without deep, prolonged, and independent study – always seeking out the original sources and developing his own views only when he had thoroughly assimilated them. It is an attitude totally foreign to secondhand acceptance of ideas. He had the best of personal reasons for taking an interest in Engels's work and occasionally referring to it, but this does not warrant the view that he fully endorsed it. There are, of course, even stronger objections to imputing to him the views on historical materialism voiced by Engels after Marx's death.

It seems justified, however, to use the works written jointly by Marx and Engels – above all, *The German Ideology* and *The Commu-: nist Manifesto* – as evidence for Marx's views. If we compare the powerful, complex arguments of the former work with Engels's contemporary writings on similar topics, it is difficult to believe that he had more than a small share of the responsibility. Similarly, if we compare the latter work with the rough draft, written by Engels alone, we must conclude that the broad historical sweep and the most penetrating formulations are due to Marx. In any case – and this is what matters – there is no reason to believe that Marx did not identify himself fully with the views expressed in the two works.

## MARXISM AFTER MARX

The development of Marx's doctrine after his death first followed the course of a mainstream, the Second International, and then divided into two separate currents, Soviet Marxism and Western Marxism. The story of these developments is, by and large, a depressing one. Although the Marxist movement has produced some great political leaders, there have been no outstanding thinkers after Marx. Moreover, the propensity of some political leaders to believe themselves great thinkers and their ability to impose this view on others have had a permanently stultifying effect on intellectual life in the communist countries. Marxists in Western Europe, on the other hand, have indulged in obscurantism, utopianism, and irresponsibility. There are nuances and exceptions, but on the whole it is difficult not to subscribe to Kolakowski's negative assessment of the development of Marxist doctrine.

The Second International was formed in 1889 as an association of (mainly European) socialist parties. For all practical purposes it broke down in 1914, when workers of different countries took to arms against each other. Whatever was left was destroyed a few years later, when the October Revolution made it evident that the carefully worked out compromise formulations did not provide any guide to hard political choices.

Politically as well as theoretically, the International was dominated by the German Socialist Party (SPD). Although its official image was that of the revolutionary spearhead of the working class, it was in reality a conservative, bureaucratic organization, oriented mainly toward its own survival and entrenchment. The sociologist Robert Michels cited the SPD as evidence for what he baptized the "iron law of oligarchy." A later historian referred to its strategy as "negative integration" and "revolutionary waiting." The leading theoretician of SPD, Karl Kautsky, was also the dominant thinker of the International, together with the Russian Georghi Plekhanov. Between them they completed the process begun by Engels – to cut the brilliant, sometimes incoherent ideas of Marx down to size and order. With some finishing touches added by Lenin, "Marxism-Leninism" – with the twin doctrines of historical materialism and dialectical materialism – was in place. It is characterized by shallow Hegelianism, naive scientism, lack of falsifiability, and a strong preference for assertion over argument. It is Marxism set in concrete.

There were other trends and figures in the International. An early revolt against the pseudorevolutionary stance of the SPD was made by Eduard Bernstein around 1900. He asserted, essentially, that revolution was unlikely, because capitalism was no longer prone to cyclical crises; superfluous, because the socialist goals could be realized by nonviolent means; and in any case undesirable, because notions like "the dictatorship of the proletariat" belong to a lower stage of civilization. Although these views largely coincided with the practices of SPD, the party was embarrassed by his voicing them in public. "Dear Ede," wrote a trade union leader, "one doesn't say these things, one simply does them."

Left-wing critics, notably Lenin and Rosa Luxemburg, wanted the International to become genuinely revolutionary. The "organizational question" is central in their writings. Marx had never developed a theory of organization, except for the general remark that "the emancipation of the working classes must be conquered by the working classes themselves," because the opposite view runs into the problem that "the educator must himself be educated." To Lenin's mind, this attitude was sheer romanticism. With relentless pragmatism, he insisted on a centralized and hierarchical organization of the workers – what came to be known as "democratic centralism." Rosa Luxemburg, on the other hand, tried to work out the implications of Marx's views, toward a working-class movement that was both spontaneous and revolutionary. She was the first great "activist" of the socialist movement – precursor and heroine of May 1968 but with a more serious bent than the flower generation. She is the only one of the great socialist leaders in the West to have been killed in revolutionary action, in Berlin after the end of World War I.

Luxemburg was also one of the best analytical minds of the Second International. The crispness and freshness of her political writings strike one even today, although her more self-conscious theoretical efforts are distinctly forgettable. An even more impressive thinker was Leon Trotsky. Like Marx, and like Luxemburg, he suffered from wishful thinking and lack of intellectual discipline, but he also had a rare grasp of history and political sociology, which enabled him to adapt Marx's theory of revolution to backward nations. It can be argued, however, that history has shown him right to a greater extent than he hoped for, by suggesting that revolutions will occur only in the countries on the periphery of capitalism, without spreading to the core countries.

The further history of Marxism in the communist countries resembles that of any other "degenerating research programme," to use a phrase from Imre Lakatos. The development of the theory took the form of Ptolemaic additions to save appearances, ad hoc hypotheses to explain anomalies, tortuous exegeses, and stubborn disregard of facts. It was accompanied by total destruction of philosophy, with the partial exception of logical theory; by near-total paralysis of the social sciences; and by a severe setback for the natural sciences, notably in genetics. The destruction of reason that took place under Stalin or during the Chinese Cultural Revolution had no precedent in history. The recovery is still incomplete or uncertain, except in the natural sciences.

The causal role of Marxism-Leninism in these developments remains unclear. The rise of the pseudogeneticist Lysenko was probably due more to his proletarian background and to the immense faith in the power of science to bring rapid results that characterized the Soviet state in the first years than to any "dialectical" features of his views. Indeed, by virtue of its essential vagueness dialectical materialism lends itself to the justification, after the fact, of virtually any theory. Whereas some argued that dialectical *materialism* requires genes to have a specific material substrate, others asserted that *dialectical* materialism, as opposed to mechanical materialism, requires them to be lodged in the organism as a whole. Whether the choice between these views was decided on scientific grounds or on political, the philosophical justification was mainly a ritual embellishment.

Most forms of Western Marxism can be characterized as attempts to create a synthesis of Marx and various other thinkers. Its inception was marked by the publication of Georg Lukacs's *History and Class Consciousness* in 1923. This work anticipates in a quite remarkable way the Hegelian reinterpretation of Marx that was fully launched a few years later, with the publication of Marx's early manuscripts. Lukacs was also influenced by the writings of Max Weber; in particular, his interpretation of Marx's notion of alienation owes much to Weber's idea of the increasing rationalization of society. In spite of many valuable insights in this and other works, Lukacs's career as a whole can be summarized as the abdication of reason or, in Kolakowski's phrase, reason in the service of dogma. The political and intellectual irresponsibility of his work is matched only by the fascination that for a long time he exerted on other Western intellectuals. Like Pascal with regard to religion, they argued that in politics "il n'y a rien de si conforme à la raison que ce désaveu de la raison."

Within the same intellectual orbit we may also mention figures like Karl Mannheim or Karl Korsch. More durably influential, however, was the "Frankfurt School." Counted among its original members were Herbert Marcuse, Max Horkheimer, and Theodor von Adorno; the central contemporary descendant is Jürgen Habermas. Theirs was a synthesis not of Marx and Weber but of Marx and Freud — two great unmaskers, debunkers, and would-be liberators. Much of the work of the early Frankfurt School is marred, however, by Hegelian obscurantism and thinly disguised elitism. Again the reader is referred to Kolakowski for a devastating review. The work of Habermas is also somewhat impenetrable but more solidly founded in rational argument.

French Marxism has been through two major phases. The first

was dominated by Jean-Paul Sartre and Maurice Merleau-Ponty, who added Husserl and Heidegger to the prisms through which Marx could be read. It is somewhat inaccurate, however, to refer to this school as "existential Marxism," because the major work it produced — Sartre's *Critique of Dialectical Reason* — owes less to existential philosophy than to French economic and political historians. The second phase arose through the improbable and barren marriage of Marx with Ferdinand de Saussure, the founder of structural linguistics. In the interpretation of Louis Althusser, scientism again came to the forefront in Marxism, after a generation of Marxists who had insisted that the categories of natural science were inapplicable to the study of society.

English Marxism: Is there such a thing? Marx himself grew increasingly cross with his adopted country, deploring the crude empiricism of the English and their lack of revolutionary fervor. The Hegelian aspects of Marxism certainly never took hold in England or in the United States. Marxian political economy, which did not much interest the Continental Marxists, had stronger appeal. Joan Robinson's *Accumulation of Capital* from 1956 was perhaps the most important work in Marxist economic theory after Marx, although it turned out to create an orthodoxy of its own that has become a serious obstacle to progress. Other recent Anglo-American work in Marxist philosophy, history, and social science is more promising — at least in my opinion, because I am referring to the tendency that has shaped the present exposition. The work of G. A. Cohen, John Roemer, and others unites rigor and relevance in a way that has been sorely lacking in Marxism.

There is, finally, the Marxism of the Third World countries. This has largely been concerned with extending Marx's notion of exploitation from the national to the international domain. Examples include the dependency theory of André Gunder Frank, the theory of unequal exchange proposed by Aghiri Emmanuel, and Samir Amin's theory of accumulation on a world scale. Though often suggestive, these writings are with few exceptions flawed by technical deficiencies and conceptual naiveté.

Because these writers do not in these respects compare unfavorably with, say, Horkheimer or Althusser, this comment ought not to be taken as a slur on their Third World origin. The problem is that Marxism tends to attract thinkers who are either fascinated by the darkly Hegelian origins of the theory or – on the other extreme – urgently preoccupied with practical relevance. Often the extremes meet, in an unnerving combination of extremely abstract theory and highly specific proposals. What Marxism needs is the development of what Robert Merton called "theories of the middle range." For this purpose it may be necessary – indeed, in the present phase it is necessary – to think less about relevance in the short term, to become more relevant in the long term. When Marx went into his inner exile in the British Museum, he followed the strategy "One step backward, two steps forward," taking time off from politics to fashion a tool that could then be of use in politics. The theory he developed has done service for a century but is becoming increasingly irrelevant for most of our urgent problems. "Back to the British Museum!" is hardly a slogan with mass political appeal, but it is one that Marxists would do well to ponder.

## EDITIONS OF MARX'S WRITINGS

In German and English, there are four editions of Marx's and Engels's collected works, none of them complete. There are also numerous editions of individual writings, a few of which are mentioned below.

There are two different editions, each of them intended as the definitive scholarly edition, referred to as *Marx–Engels Gesamt-Ausgabe (MEGA)*. The first *MEGA* was published between 1927 and 1935. Before it was stopped by Stalin's rise to power, it had transformed Marx scholarship and Marxist thought through the publication of *The Economic and Philosophical Manuscripts* and *The German Ideology*.

The next edition, in chronological order, is the *Marx–Engels Werke (MEW)*, published in East Berlin from 1956. It is the only edition that is approximately complete, but it is not a scholarly edition. Marx's writings in English and French are published in German translation. Many of the posthumous economic writings are not included here; some works also appear to have been excluded on ideological grounds. The editorial introductions and notes are heavily dogmatic but provide much useful information.

An English translation of *MEW* has been in progress since the 1970s, as Karl Marx and Friedrich Engels, *Collected Works* (*CW*). It appears to aim at completeness but not at scholarship; yet it is invaluable to Marx scholars because much of the English journalism here becomes easily accessible in the original language for the first time.

Finally, the second *MEGA* has been unfolding since 1977 at a majestic pace and will not come to a halt until well into the next century. It has already brought us several major unpublished manuscripts, notably the previously unknown parts of the 1861–3 *Critique*. More preparatory manuscripts for *Capital* will follow. The scholarly apparatus is splendid, but the editors have not felt able to avoid the usual ideological rituals.

The standard German editions of the three volumes of *Capital* are identical with volumes 23–5 of *MEW*. An English translation of the first volume appeared in 1886, authorized by Engels. All later editions have been reprinted of this translation, until a new translation by Ben Fowkes was published by Penguin in 1976. Being as reliable as the original translation and less encumbered by heavy Victorian prose, it ought eventually to replace it as the standard English reference. Yet for many years to come many will continue to read the three volumes in the edition published by International Publishers, as this is the one usually cited by English scholars.

The 1953 German edition of the *Grundrisse* has now been superseded by the publication in the new *MEGA*. An English translation by Martin Nicolaus was published by Penguin in 1973. The standard German edition of the *Theories of Surplus-Value* used to be volumes 26.1–26.3 of the *MEW*, but these are also superseded by the new *MEGA*. The standard English translation is published by Lawrence and Wishart. *The Results of the Immediate Process of Production* is translated as an appendix to the Penguin edition of *Capital I*; an easily accessible German edition was published by Verlag Neue Kritik (Frankfurt) in 1969, itself a photographic reprint of the 1933 Moscow edition.

## Bibliography

There are many books entitled "Marx on . . . " or "Marx and Engels on . . . ," collecting their writings and obiter dicta on various topics. There are also many selections of their writings from different periods: the early manuscripts, the American journalism, writings from the First International, and so on. There are various "Selected Writings" covering the corpus as a whole and there are, of course, many editions of most individual writings. It is impossible to list them all, and there is not much point in selecting a few. If one should be singled out, it is Saul Padover's edition of *The Letters of Karl Marx*, (Prentice-Hall, 1979), which usefully collects the most important correspondence. Besides providing valuable supplementary sources for the understanding of his theories, Marx's letters vividly convey his ebullient personality.

BIBLIOGRAPHY

*Introduction.* By far the best guide to the Marxist universe is Leszek Kolakowski's *Main Currents of Marxism*, 3 vols. (Oxford University Press, 1978). It is excellent on philosophy, superb on politics, but somewhat scanty on social theory, especially economics.

*Life and writings.* There is no first-rate, full-length biography or intellectual biography of Marx comparable to those of Rosa Luxemburg or Leon Trotsky cited below. An excellent short study is Isaiah Berlin's *Karl Marx*, 3d ed. (Oxford University Press, 1973). Maximilien Rubel's *Karl Marx: Essai de Biographie Intellectuelle* (Presses Universitaires de France, 1959) remains useful. A clear biographical presentation is David McLellan, *Karl Marx: His Life and Thought* (Macmillan, 1973). More ambitious, with deeper psychological understanding, is Jerrold Seigel, *Marx's Fate: The Shape of a Life* (Princeton University Press, 1978). On Marx's Jewishness, see Julius Carlebach, *Karl Marx and the Radical Critique of Judaism* (Routledge and Kegan Paul, 1978) and Isaiah Berlin, "Benjamin Disraeli, Karl Marx, and the search for identity," in his *Against the Current* (Viking Press, 1980). Two books on Marx as a politician are Oscar J. Hammen, *The Red '48ers: Karl Marx and Friedrich Engels* (Scribner, 1969), and Henry Collins and Chimen Abramsky, *Karl Marx and the British Labour Movement* (Macmillan, 1965). Marx's relation to the anarchists is discussed in Pierre Ansart, *Marx et l'Anarchisme* (Presses Universitaires de France, 1969), and in Paul Thomas, *Karl Marx and the Anarchists* (Routledge and Kegan Paul, 1980). An encyclopedic survey of Marx's stylistic repertoire is S. S. Prawer, *Karl Marx and World Literature* (Oxford University Press, 1978).

*Marx and Engels.* A work especially devoted to the relation between Marx and Engels is Norman Levine, *The Tragic Deception: Marx contra Engels* (Clio Books, 1975). A briefer treatment is that of Gareth Stedman Jones, "Engels and the history of Marxism," in Eric Hobsbawm (ed.), *The History of Marxism* (Harvester Press, 1982), 1:290–326.

*Marxism after Marx.* The three volumes of Kolakowski's *Main Currents of Marxism* are indispensable. They can be usefully supplemented by volumes 3 to 5 of G. D. H. Cole's *History of Socialist Thought* (Macmillan, 1953–60). A good introduction to Soviet Marxism and its historical sources is Z. A. Jordan, *The Evolution of Dialectical Materialism* (Macmillan, 1967). It can be usefully supplemented by Loren Graham, *Science and Philosophy in the Soviet Union* (Knopf, 1972). A history of the SPD is Dieter Groh, *Negative Integration und revolutionärer Attentismus* (Suhrkamp, 1973). Valuable studies of individual figures are J. P. Nettl, *Rosa Luxemburg* (Oxford University Press, 1966), and B. Knei-Paz, *The Social and Political Thought of Leon Trotsky* (Oxford University Press, 1977). On the Frankfurt School, see Martin Jay, *The Dialectical Imagination* (Little, Brown, 1973). There is, to my knowledge, no good treatment of French Marxism.

*Editions of Marx's writings.* A useful survey is that of Eric Hobsbawm, "The fortune of Marx's and Engels' writings," in E. Hobsbawm (ed.), *History of Marxism,* 1: 327–344.

## 2

# MARXIST METHODOLOGY

## INTRODUCTION

MANY claims have been made for "the Marxist method." Some of them are justified, others are exaggerated, false, or unintelligible. Although Marx had valuable methodological insights that are not yet fully exhausted, there is no "dialectical reason" that separates Marxists from ordinary mortals. On first exposure to Marxist writings, many feel mystified and terrorized by references to the "dialectical unity of opposites," the "revolutionary unity of theory and practice," and similar phrases. All too often, such locutions have allowed followers of Marx to get away with murder, sometimes literally so. It is against this background of extreme self-indulgence that I adopt what may look like an excessively purist viewpoint on methodology. Readers may tolerate suggestive ambiguity in a writer if on past performance they are willing to give him the benefit of doubt, but Marxism has long since exhausted its credit.

The Marxist methodology that I want emphatically to reject is an amalgam of three elements. The first is methodological holism, the view that in social life there exist wholes or collectivities, statements about which cannot be reduced to statements about the member individuals. The second is functional explanation, the attempt to explain social phenomena in terms of their beneficial consequences for someone or something, even when no intention to bring about these consequences has been demonstrated. The third is dialectical deduction, a mode of thinking that is derived from Hegel's *Logic* and that does not lend itself to brief summary.

Of these, the first two are also found, separately or in combination, in non-Marxist social science. Emile Durkheim, among oth-

21

ers, insisted that, even were psychology to become a perfect science, there would remain some social facts it could not explain. Robert Merton has advocated explanation of institutions and behavioral patterns in terms of their "latent functions," that is, consequences that were neither intended by the agents who produce them nor perceived by those who benefit from them. Social anthropologists have proposed explanations that are both holistic and functional. When Marx employs the same method, he differs not only in the Hegelian element sometimes superimposed on it but also in the nature of the wholes and the benefits that enter into the explanation. Most importantly, he uses functional explanation not only to account for the stability of societies but also to demonstrate their inherent tendency to develop toward communism.

Marx was very much a nineteenth-century figure, which is to say that in methodological matters he was a transitional figure. He had liberated himself from explicit theological assumptions, yet he retained the teleological outlook they had inspired. Like most of his contemporaries he was impressed by the progress of biology and wrongly thought that the study of society could profit from the study of organisms. (It is only fair to add, however, that he indulged much less in analogical inference from biology than, say, Auguste Comte or Herbert Spencer.) His scientism – the belief that there exist "laws of motion" for society that operate with "iron necessity" – rested on a naive extrapolation from the achievements of natural science. We shall find, over and over again, that dated methodological conceptions coexist, in his work, with strikingly fresh insights.

## METHODOLOGICAL INDIVIDUALISM

Methodological individualism is the view that all institutions, behavioral patterns, and social processes can in principle be explained in terms of individuals only: their actions, properties, and relations. It is a form of reductionism, which is to say that it enjoins us to explain complex phenomena in terms of their simpler components. Reductionism is a central strategy in science. It has created such disciplines as molecular biology and physical chemistry. The case of biology is especially interesting, because for a

22

long time it was claimed to be inherently irreducible to physics or chemistry. A similar claim is still made today with respect to the social sciences. The counterclaim is not that there already exists a social psychology or psychological sociology that has effectuated a complete reduction. Rather, it is that there is no objection in principle to such a reduction being carried out, even though it may remain impracticable for the foreseeable future. One may add that with respect to some problems the "search for microfoundations" – another term for methodological individualism – has already yielded important results. A full reduction is possible in principle; a partial reduction is well under way.

This is not the place to defend the doctrine of methodological individualism, beyond saying that our confidence in and understanding of an explanation is improved if we open "the black box" and get a look at the nuts and bolts, the cogs and wheels of the mechanism inside it. Some objections may in any case evaporate if a few things are made clear. First, the doctrine has no implications about the kind of individual-level explanation that is needed to carry out the reduction. In particular, the assumption that individuals are rational and selfish is not part of the doctrine, although compatible with it. Second, it does not assume that individuals are "atoms" that have a presocial existence before they come together to form society. Relations between individuals must be let in on the ground floor of social explanation. Third, it does not extend to what goes on inside peoples' heads. In the phrase "The United States fears the Soviet Union," the first collective noun is subject to reduction but not the second, because what the individual Americans fear may well be a nebulous collective entity.

Lastly, adherence to methodological individualism should not blind one to the dangers of premature reductionism. An important example is the following. To understand successful collective action, such as a strike, we would ideally like to give an account in terms of the motives and beliefs of the participants. These proximate causes of the behavior are, however, usually very elusive. Often the remote causes are more tractable. We may, for instance, be able to establish a causal connection between, on the one hand, certain features of the group in question and, on the other hand, its propensity to strike. Other things being equal, a strike may be more likely the more similar the background of the members and the more stable the composition of the group. We know that the effect of these remote "macrovariables" must be mediated by their impact on individual motives and beliefs, but we may be unable to specify the mechanism. In such cases the search for microfoundations may lead to barren speculation. The principle of methodological individualism says only that the search is not inherently sterile, although, in any given case, it may well be pointless in the present state of knowledge.

In Marx there are two main instances of methodological holism, corresponding to his two central theoretical concerns. In the analysis of capitalism, "Capital" appears as a collective entity, which cannot be reduced to the several individual firms. Marx believed that capital had a logic of its own, which was somehow prior in the explanatory order to market behavior and competition. According to methodological individualism, on the other hand, any "laws of motion and self-regulation" of capitalism must be deduced as theorems from axioms specifying the motives and constraints of firms, workers, and consumers.

In historical materialism, "Humanity" appears as the collective subject whose flowering in communism is the final goal of history. Marx was strongly influenced by Hegel's tripartite division of history into an initial undifferentiated unity, followed by a phase of conflict and alienation and culminating with a higher unity that retains the individuality developed in the second phase. In Hegel's and Marx's secular theology, mankind had to alienate itself from itself in order to regain itself in an enriched form. Exactly how this is mediated by the actions of individuals, motivated by goals of their own, is never made clear.

The point should not be overemphasized. Marx was not a purely speculative social thinker. Most of the time he was indeed concerned with forging links among individual motives, individual behavior, and aggregate consequences. On the other hand, one should not go to the other extreme and view his references to Capital and Mankind as rhetorical devices with no explanatory relevance. Marx does often point to the needs of these collective entities in order to explain events and institutions that appear as if by magic to fulfill them. His belief in the independent logic of

24

aggregates does sometimes weaken his motivation to study the fine grain of social structure and social change. Speculative elements coexist, often within the same work, with more soundly based views. The *Grundrisse,* in particular, shows Marx's mind operating in both registers, with dizzying transitions.

"Individualism" is a term with many connotations. Quite independently of the issues just discussed, one may profess individualism in an ethical or normative sense. This doctrine, though not in itself a substantive ethical view, imposes constraints on any such view by stipulating that in the final analysis only individuals are morally relevant. Some implications of this view are the following. The advancement of knowledge, the creation of great works of art, or the protection of nature are not independent sources of value – they have value only to the extent that they are valued by individuals. Equality between the sexes, between classes, or between nations is not a value in itself – it is to be promoted only to the extent that it leads to greater equality between individuals. It is never justified to ask people to sacrifice themselves for the sake of the fatherland or the proletariat – unless one can show that other concrete individuals benefit. (And even then, of course, the justification may be dubious.)

Marx was an individualist in this normative sense. He appreciated that class societies in general and capitalism in particular had led to enormous advances in civilization, as judged by the best achievements in art and science. Yet this process was the self-realization of Man rather than of individual men, who had, for the most part, lived in misery. Indeed, only by the exploitation of the many could class societies create the free time in which a few could contribute to the progress of civilization. The attraction of communism in his eyes was to allow the self-realization of each and every individual, not just of a small elite. As a by-product there will also be an unprecedented flowering of mankind, but this is not, to repeat, in itself a source of value.

## MARXISM AND RATIONAL CHOICE

That human behavior can be explained in terms of rational choice is becoming a central, perhaps even dominant view in the social sciences. Broadly speaking, it was born around 1870 when the marginalist revolution in economic theory allowed a precise formulation of the costs and benefits attached to alternative uses of scarce resources. *Capital I* was published in 1867, so we would not expect Marx to have been exposed to these ideas. Yet we may ask whether his theory is consistent with the basic assumptions of the rational-choice approach, or whether − as later followers and opponents have claimed − the two are mutually incompatible.

The explanation of an action makes appeal to two successive filtering processes. From the whole set of abstractly possible courses of action we first filter out those that do not satisfy the given logical, physical, economic, or mental constraints. Human beings cannot have their cake and eat it too; they cannot fly in the air like birds; they cannot spend more than they earn; and they cannot act like lightning-fast calculating machines. Within the remaining set we appeal to some principle of selection that explains which action is finally realized. Rational-choice theory assumes that people will choose the course of action they prefer, or think is best. To act rationally is to choose the best action in the feasible set.

The full structure of rational-choice theory is more complex than one would glean from this stark statement. Here are some of the qualifications that need to be added. First, although the standard theory presents constraints and preferences as independent of each other, either can in fact be shaped by the other. The constraints are shaped by the preferences if the person decides ahead of time to eliminate certain options from the feasible set, which one might do to avoid temptation or − more paradoxically − to improve a bargaining position. Conversely, preferences are shaped by constraints if the person consciously or unconsciously adapts what he wants to what he can get. Second, it ought to be emphasized that the theory says that the person will choose the action which he thinks is best suited to his purposes, which is not to say that it is the best in a more objective sense. Rational-choice explanation embodies a claim about the relation among action, motives, and beliefs. It differs in this respect from evolutionary explanation in biology, which asserts that organisms end up having the features that are objectively best from the point of view of their fitness. Third, it often happens that several people simultaneously try to adjust rationally to each other. This belongs to the realm of *game theory*, as it has somewhat unfortunately come to be known. A better name would have been *the theory of interdependent decisions*. I shall say more about game theory later.

First, however, we may go back to the two filters, to see what alternatives to rational-choice theory might look like. Some would deny that there is more than one filter operating. They would argue that the constraints tend to be so strong as to eliminate all alternatives but one, so that nothing is left for the second filter to operate on. This view may be plausible in some cases. For workers in classical capitalism, for instance, the joint effect of the budget constraint and the calorie–protein constraint may have been to narrow the feasible consumption purchases to a very small set. As a general theory, however, this "structuralist" view is implausible. It is hard to think of a general mechanism that would shape the constraints so as to leave the agents with exactly one option. It will not do, for example, to say that the members of the ruling class make it their business to restrict the feasible set of the exploited class, because this statement assumes that the former class has the very freedom of choice it denies to the latter.[1]

Another class of alternatives proposes different mechanisms in the second filter. There are two main contenders. On the one hand, there is the sociological view that men are governed by social norms, roles, habit, or tradition. The view implies that behavior is less sensible to changes in the feasible set than one would expect on the rational-choice approach. Value is attached to specific forms of behavior as such, not only to their outcomes. On the other hand, there is the view that people do not choose what is best, only what in some sense is good enough. (By a neologism, this view is known as the "satisficing" theory of choice, as opposed to the "maximizing" assumption of rational-choice theory.) The argument is that the costs of collecting and evaluating information, as well as the uncertainty surrounding the value of information, make nonsense of the notion of "optimal behavior."

1 In any case, a rational ruling class would leave the exploited class with some freedom of choice. It would restrict the set of alternatives up to the point where the element preferred within it by the members of the exploited class is also the one which the ruling class prefers within the unrestricted set.

There is a good deal to each of these views. If in my opinion they have not succeeded in dethroning rational-choice theory from its dominant position, it is because they lack robustness and predictive power. The facts they invoke in their support are real enough, but as is generally acknowledged by philosophers of science, "Facts don't kick." To discredit a theory it is not sufficient to adduce facts that count against it; one must also produce another, better explanation. As long as the sociological theory does not specify the limits within which behavior will remain unaffected by changes in the feasible set, or the satisficing theory does not come up with an explanation of why people have different ideas of what is good enough, they will not be able to claim superiority. These theories offer what is sometimes called thick description, not explanation.

There is a further response to rational-choice theory that does not quite coincide with any of these alternatives. It goes as follows: True, action can be explained in terms of the preferences and beliefs of the actors, but this is not a rock-bottom explanation. Motives and beliefs are not identical across individuals or stable over time. They are shaped and modified by social forces, including deliberate manipulation. Hence, rational-choice explanation offers a shallow understanding of behavior and must be supplemented by an account of how preferences and beliefs emerge from within the social structure.

The point might appear to be trivial. It is always possible to search, beyond the cause of the phenomenon, for the cause of the cause. One cannot on each occasion go back to first causes. Yet, for someone who, like the Marxist, wants to understand long-term historical trends, it points to a real difficulty. In the long run nothing can be taken for constant or given; everything must be explained from within or "endogenously." It is probably true to say that this is one of the main unresolved problems of the social sciences. True, we do know something about how beliefs and preferences are shaped by social structure. In particular, there is good evidence for the view that people adjust their desires or their beliefs so as to reduce "cognitive dissonance," that is, the mental tension that arises when what one values is also believed to be out of reach. The oppressed often end up accepting their state, because the alternative is too hard to live with. Yet we know little about the limits within which this mechanism operates and beyond which revolt becomes a real possibility.

I promised to say a few words about game theory. I am among those who believe game theory offers a unifying conceptual framework for most of social science, in that it enables us to understand three kinds of interdependencies that pervade social life. There is, first, the fact that the reward of each depends on the rewards of all, by altruism, envy, and the like; second, the fact that the reward of each depends on the choices of all, through general social causality; and, third, the fact that the choice of each depends on the choices of all, through anticipation and strategic calculation. This is not to say that we can observe each kind of interdependency in each case of social action. They represent conceptual possibilities, not necessities.

Game theory has analyzed numerous forms of social interaction. Here I shall only spell out the structure of the most prominent among them, the so-called Prisoner's Dilemma, which is one of the most intensively studied problems in contemporary social science. Rather than retell the anecdote that lent its name to the dilemma, I shall illustrate it by sticking to the example of strikes. Let us assume that each worker has the choice between two options: to join the strike or to abstain. Let us assume, moreover, that it is better for all workers if all strike than if none do, because in the former case they can successfully press for a wage raise. Let us assume, finally, that the workers are solely motivated by personal material gains. Then, for each worker it is always better to abstain, regardless of what others do. If they strike, he or she can act as a free rider and get the wage rise without the risk and cost involved in striking. If they do not, there is no point in a unilateral act of solidarity. Hence the individual will not strike; nor, because they are similarly placed, will the others. The result of all workers acting in an individually rational way is that the outcome is worse for all than it could have been had they been able to cooperate. This is also often referred to as the free-rider problem.

The main source of Marxist resistance to rational-choice theory is the first, "structuralist" objection. Marx often emphasizes that workers and capitalists are not agents in the full sense of the term:

free, active choosers. Rather, they are mere placeholders or, as he put it, "economic character masks," condemned to act out the logic of the capitalist system. Workers are forced to sell their labor power, and the idea that they have a free choice in the labor market is an ideological construction. As consumers, their choice between different consumption plans is restricted by low wages. Similarly, capitalists are forced by competition to act as they do, including the inhumane practices of exploitation. If they tried to behave differently, they would be wiped out.

This argument fails because the notions of choice and force are not incompatible. Consider two situations. In one, workers have two options: barely surviving as independent peasants and barely surviving as workers. In the other, the first option is the same, but the other is now to work for a wage that allows a good standard of living. In the latter case, the workers are forced to sell their labor power — not by coercion but by what Marx calls the force of circumstances. In the former, the workers clearly have a choice between two options. But if they have a choice in the first situation, they must also have one in the second; the existence of choice cannot be removed by improving one of the options. A somewhat different argument establishes the reality of capitalist choice in a competitive market. When capitalists, under the pressure of competition, survey alternative modes of action and go through extensive calculation to find the most profitable, they engage in the very paradigm of choice behavior. The fact that they do not survive if they make the wrong choice does not mean that they do not make choices; on the contrary, choice is presupposed.

In Marx's economic theory the denial of choice is closely linked with the labor theory of value. Marx postulated that the economy had a surface structure and a deep structure. The surface structure is that of everyday economic life, in which the economic agents make rational choices in terms of the market prices of goods. In the deep structure, goods are characterized by their labor values — the amount of socially necessary labor time required to produce them. The surface structure is merely the working out of the relations defined by the deep structure, just as the visible appearance of a physical object is a mere consequence of its atomic structure. I shall argue later that this theory of the relation between values and prices, the essence and the appearance in economic life, is barely intelligible. It certainly misled Marx, in preventing him from appreciating the centrality of choice and alternatives in economics.

Outside economic analysis proper Marx's structuralist method did not affect his concrete investigations. In the brilliant core chapters on economic sociology in *Capital I*, Marx fully recognized the subtle interplay among entrepreneurial choice, profit, technology, and power in the firm. His political sociology likewise was sensitive to rational and strategic thinking on the part of the main actors. I should add, however, that in both cases there is one obstacle to a purely rational-choice interpretation of these texts. This is his tendency to deploy functional explanation, in which events and institutions are explained on the grounds that they are better for some agent or agents but not necessarily on the grounds that they are chosen because they are better.

## FUNCTIONAL EXPLANATION IN MARXISM

Functional explanation is puzzling and controversial, for reasons that may be brought out by comparing it with other modes of scientific explanation. In causal explanation, we account for a phenomenon by citing its (actual) cause, assumed to have preceded it in time. In intentional explanation, of which rational-choice explanation is the most important variety, we cite the intended consequences of the phenomenon. Again the intention occurs at an earlier time than the thing we want to explain by citing it. In functional explanation, we cite the actual consequence of the phenomenon in order to account for it. Marx, for instance, explains upward social mobility by pointing to the economic benefits the capitalist class derives from having a steady stream of fresh recruits. The puzzle is how an event can be explained by another event that occurs at a later time. There must be an explanation for the event when it happens — it cannot be necessary to await the consequences in order to explain it.

The most plausible solution to this puzzle is to deny that functional explanation can account for single events or processes. For something to be a proper object of functional explanation, it must be a pattern of similar, recurring events. Let me give an example, cited only for the sake of illustration and not because I believe the story it tells is true. If in a given capitalist society we observe upward social mobility as a regular phenomenon, so that in each generation some workers become self-employed or small capitalists, this pattern could be explained by the benefits provided to the capitalist class, in the following way. Upward mobility in one generation contributes to the economic vitality and prosperity of capitalism. A prosperous system provides further opportunities for mobility in the next generation. Moreover, that capitalism is seen to deliver the goods provides it with legitimacy and channels individual aspirations into desires for mobility within the system rather than revolt against it. The opportunity and the desire for mobility come together in creating, or re-creating, actual mobility. Hence, upward mobility at one point in time has consequences that lead to the continued presence of mobility at a later time.

The example shows that functional explanation involves a *feedback loop*, a causal connection from the consequences of one event of the kind we are trying to explain to another, later event of the same kind. Functional explanation is applicable when a pattern of behavior maintains itself through the consequences it generates; more specifically, through consequences that benefit some group, which may or may not be the same as the group of people displaying the behavior. In the mobility example the agents and those whom they benefit are distinct groups. An example (again used only for the sake of illustration) in which they coincide follows.

If the satisficing theory of choice is correct, firms do not and cannot consciously maximize profits. Rather, they make decisions by following rules of thumb that appear to be "good enough." In a competitive market, however, only the firms that happen to hit upon profit-maximizing rules of thumb will survive; the others will go bankrupt. We can then explain the observed behavior of firms by pointing to the beneficial consequences of their decision rules. The reason we observe these particular rules of thumb rather than others is that they maximize the profit of the firm. The pattern of explanation is similar to that of functional explanation in biology, in which we explain the optimal adaptation of organisms by appealing to chance variation and natural selection.

These two examples provide perfectly valid explanations, assuming the truth of their premises. Why, then, object so strongly to the use of functional explanation in Marxism? First, in Marx's philosophy of history we find explanations of singular, nonrecurrent events in terms of their unintended consequences. An argument of this type rests on a metaphysical impossibility. Second, in many functional explanations – within and outside Marxism – the feedback loop is not demonstrated but only postulated or tacitly assumed. This, in fact, is the major objection. In the mobility example, the suggested feedback loop is not proposed by Marx, nor does he suggest any other mechanism that could support the explanation.

The mere fact that an activity has beneficial consequences – be it for capitalist domination, for social integration, or in some other respect – is not sufficient to explain it. Any phenomenon can be shown to benefit a number of groups or interests, especially if we are allowed to vary the time perspective. For instance, Marx argued that state policies not in the short-term interest of capitalists might – precisely because of that fact – be in their long-term interest. If we grant, for the sake of argument, that this is in fact the case, we still have no explanation. This would require the exhibition of a mechanism by which the satisfaction of long-term interests generates or sustains the policies. In the absence of a demonstrated mechanism, the benefits could, for all we know, be purely accidental and hence nonexplanatory.

One important mode of Marxist explanation combines methodological holism and functional explanation by asserting that the behavior of a class can be explained by the beneficial consequences for the class members. Consider the following explanation of why technical change tends to be labor-saving rather than capital-saving. Labor-saving innovations are in the interest of Capital, because they reduce the demand for labor and hence lower the wage that workers have to be paid. The argument fails because it provides no reason why the individual capitalist firm should prefer this kind of innovation. In a competitive industry, a single firm is too small to affect the going wage rate and hence has no incentive to search for one kind of innovation rather than another. We are, in fact, dealing with an example of the free-rider problem. The argument that collectively optimal outcomes, when realized, are realized because they are collectively optimal is one of the most frequent forms of functional explanation. It has two closely related defects, in that it lacks both microfoundations and an appropriate feedback mechanism.

## DIALECTICS

"Dialectics" is a term that has been used with a number of meanings. Common to almost all is the view that conflict, antagonism, or contradiction is a necessary condition for achieving certain results. Contradiction between ideas may be a condition for reaching truth; conflict among individuals, classes, or nations may be a necessary condition for social change. This preliminary remark suggests a distinction between a dialectical method and a dialectical process, between dialectics as a feature of our thinking about the world and dialectics as a feature of the world itself. On a certain conception of dialectics, these are not alternative conceptions but complementary ones. The dialectical method reflects the dialectical character of the world. Hegel apparently believed, at least some of the time, that our views about the world have to be contradictory because the world itself contains contradictions. This view is hardly intelligible, and I shall not discuss it here.

Let us consider, therefore, the view that these are alternative conceptions. We may then define the dialectical method as the view that in order to arrive at the truth of a matter one does not proceed by slowly and patiently refining earlier conceptions, deleting what is wrong, retaining what is correct, and adding what is missing. Rather, one goes from one extreme to another, discarding what is valuable in the old view along with what ought properly to be discarded. In a third stage one may be able to achieve a more balanced view – but only because one has passed through the extremes.

William Blake, an older contemporary of Hegel, expressed this view in two succinct phrases: "Without Contraries is no Progression" and "You never know what is enough unless you know what is more than enough." Hegel used different language. Sometimes he characterized the three stages as, respectively, thesis, antithesis, and synthesis. In a different but essentially equivalent terminology he referred to them as position, negation of the position, and negation of the negation. The Hegelian terms have a fine ring to them, but the phenomena they refer to are only the commonplace ones just described. Even if Hegel wanted to advocate a special "dialectical logic," what remains valuable in his view can be expressed in everyday language and logic. To be valuable, however, it should not be understood as asserting that this three-stage process characterizes all thinking, or that it is likely to yield better results than other procedures. Intellectual development does not always proceed from one extreme to another, and when it does truth need not benefit.

Dialectical processes in the world have similar stages. The most important example of a dialectical process in Hegel and Marx is probably the following three-step sequence, briefly mentioned earlier. Society, they argued, begins as a primitive, undifferentiated community. Persons are essentially similar to one another, without distinctive character traits or different productive functions. The community dominates the individual, who is left with little scope for free choice or individual self-realization. The next stage, the negation of the first one, occurs with the emergence of alienation (Hegel) or of class societies (Marx). It is characterized by an extreme development of individuality and by an equally extreme disintegration of community. The third stage, the negation of the negation, restores community without, however, destroying individuality. It is in this respect the synthesis of the two previous stages.

This vision had a very powerful grip on Marx's mind. It shaped his view of world history, his conception of political struggle and tactics, his image of the communist society. It is related both to methodological holism and to functional explanation, sharing, therefore, the flaws of both. In other cases, however, three-stage dialectical processes are less controversial. Consider, for instance, the development from the naive religious belief of the child, through a stage of doubt and despair, to the reflective belief of the mature person. It is certainly arguable that the direct passage from the first to the third stage is impossible. Even more plausibly, there is no going back from the third stage to the first. If we regard these as the salient features of the negation of the negation, it appears as a common although far from universal pattern. There is no "law" of the negation of the negation, but the concept has a certain value in directing our attention to problems we might otherwise have overlooked.

There is no real connection between negation of the negation as a feature of thought processes and negation of the negation as a feature of historical processes. There is no reason, that is, why the study of a three-stage dialectical process is more likely than other intellectual developments to proceed in three dialectical stages. In any case I insist on the very limited interest of dialectics – in thought or in reality – as conceived in this manner. It does not yield an operational method that can be applied with a promise of good results within well-defined boundaries, nor does it yield substantive laws of historical development with definite predictions for concrete cases. A cluster of vague, suggestive ideas, it does not offer scientific tools with analytical cutting edges.

There is, however, another acceptance of the term "dialectics" in which it does offer exactly that. It involves taking seriously, indeed literally, the idea that the world contains contradictions. To see that this view does not also involve *us* in contradictions, consider the following propositions:

1. John Smith believes that it rains.
2. John Smith believes that it does not rain.
3. John Smith does not believe that it rains.

If we assert propositions 1 and 2 simultaneously, we make a statement to the effect that the world contains contradictions. If we assert 1 and 3 simultaneously, we make a contradictory statement. This shows that a statement asserting the existence of contradictions is not itself contradictory. This observation naturally provokes three queries. One might ask, first, how propositions 1 and 2 could ever obtain simultaneously. It is true that we do not often observe this extreme form of contradictory belief systems, but there are many less extreme cases of people entertaining beliefs from which a logical contradiction can be derived. When people believed in the possibility of trisecting the angle by using only ruler and compass, they believed in something that involves a logical contradiction – although it took a lot of hard work by mathematicians to show that this was so.

One might also ask, secondly, whether the appeal to such contradictory beliefs helps us understand the world better or whether they are just a psycho-logical curiosity. To answer, let me change the example. Propositions 1 through 3 could also have been stated in terms of the desire for rain; hence, I shall give an example that involves contradictory desires rather than contradictory beliefs. I shift the ground not because I believe contradictory belief systems are trivial but because focusing on desires allows me to consider one of the best-known examples of dialectical reasoning in the history of thought, Hegel's master–slave analysis in *The Phenomenology of Spirit,* or rather an extremely simplified version of that analysis.

The contradictory desire Hegel finds in the master is the desire for a unilateral recognition. The master wants to be recognized by the slave, but he does not want to recognize the slave in return. This constellation of desires is contradictory because recognition, to be worth anything, must come from someone who is worth recognizing. What most of us value highly is recognition by competent others – by those whom we ourselves recognize. To be recognized by someone whom we pay to lavish us with praise can at most give a fleeting satisfaction; it is like transferring money from one pocket to another, not like receiving an additional income. Although strange, such strivings play an important part in human behavior. Ideas that derive from – or are very similar to – Hegel's analysis have been applied in studies ranging from American negro slavery to pathological family interactions.

One might then ask, thirdly, what all this has to do with Marx. To answer, we must move from the psychological contradictions considered so far to the realm of social contradictions. Let me begin with an example that was made famous by John Maynard Keynes but is already in Marx. It is a central paradox of capitalism that each capitalist wants his workers to have low wages, because this is good for his profits; yet he wants the workers employed by all other capitalists to have high wages, because this creates a demand for his products. Each capitalist, in other words, wants to be in a position which, for purely logical reasons, not everyone can occupy. Although the desire of each capitalist is internally consistent, their desires taken together are contradictory. There is no possible world in which they could all see their desires satisfied.

This is not merely a logical paradox. It is closely related to the recurring crises in the capitalist economy. To see this, take a case where loss of export markets leads to a fall in the demand for cars and hence in the profits of the car industry. Automobile producers will often react by laying off workers or by cutting their wages. For simplicity, consider only the second response. From their local point of view, the behavior of the firms is quite rational; yet it also has consequences for other firms, because part of the demand for their products comes from automobile workers. These firms will, in a similarly rational response, also impose lower wages, thereby hurting everybody else in the same way as they were themselves hurt by the car producers. The end result of this vicious circle can be a state of mass unemployment.

At each stage in this process a firm, by reducing wages, achieves three things. It increases the profit margin on each product that it sells. It slightly lowers the demand for its own product, because part of that demand comes from the wages of workers employed in the firm. With few exceptions, the first effect will dominate the second, so that the firm does behave rationally in cutting wages. (Henry Ford was wrong when he said that he had to pay his workers well because otherwise they could not afford to buy his cars.) By the same token the wage cut also leads to a slightly lower demand for the products made by other firms. When all firms face this situation, we have a Prisoner's Dilemma. It would be better for all firms if all abstained from reducing wages, but any given firm will always see wage cuts as an attractive proposition.

Marx was a pioneer in the study of social contradictions. Before him, many writers had been fascinated by the fact that history is "the result of human action, not of human design" (Adam Ferguson). Bernard Mandeville's *Fable of the Bees* is perhaps the first clear statement of this theme, which was later developed by, among others, Adam Smith and Hegel. Yet in these writers there is no clear analysis of the structure of unintended consequences such as was provided by Marx. In his hands it was transformed from a general *Weltanschauung* into a precision tool for the study of social change. This was his most important methodological achievement.

In addition to these two versions of Marxist dialectics – the theory of the negation of the negation and the theory of social contradictions – there is what I referred to earlier as *dialectical deduction*. In the *Grundrisse* and in the opening chapters of *Capital I,* Marx attempts to deduce the main economic categories from one another in a manner inspired by Hegel's procedure in *The Science of Logic*. In that work Hegel argued that the most general metaphysical categories are inherently unstable. The notion of being, for instance, is apparently the most universal of all categories, so universal that it is in fact empty and hence turns into its opposite, nothing. Marx argues, similarly, that the concept of money has an inherent tendency to develop into capital. Money, to preserve itself, must multiply itself – it must create a surplus, which means that it becomes capital.

This deduction is part of a longer chain: product–commodity–exchange value–money–capital–labor. Some of these concepts also stand in a historical relation to each other: subsistence production is historically prior to production for exchange, which in turn is prior to production for profit. Although some of the transitions make sense when seen as historical developments, the purported dialectical connection is unintelligible. Concepts have no "logic of development" independently of the actions that men undertake for purposes of their own.

### BIBLIOGRAPHY

*Methodological individualism.* A clear statement of this principle is in George Homans, *The Nature of Social Science* (Harcourt, Brace and World, 1967). A classic statement of methodological holism is Emile Durkheim, *The Rules of Sociological Method;* a more recent exposition is Charles Taylor, "Interpretation and the sciences of man," *Review of Metaphysics* 25 (1971): 3–51. There are several useful discussions in May Brodbeck (ed.), *Readings in the Philosophy of the Social Sciences* (Macmillan, 1968). The need for microfoundations in Marxist economic theory is argued in John Roemer, *Analytical Foundations of Marxian Economics* (Cambridge University Press,

1981). For the distinction between the self-realization of Man and that of men, see G. A. Cohen, "Karl Marx's dialectic of labour," *Philosophy and Public Affairs* 3 (1974): 235–61.

*Marxism and rational choice.* An introduction to the basic concepts in rational-choice theory is R. D. Luce and H. Raiffa, *Games and Decisions* (Wiley, 1957). Arguments for the general applicability of the theory are found in Gary Becker, *The Economic Approach to Human Behavior* (Chicago University Press, 1976), and Raymond Boudon, *The Unintended Consequences of Social Action* (St. Martin's Press, 1979). A good introduction to the theory of "satisficing" is James March, "Bounded rationality, ambiguity, and the engineering of choice," *Bell Journal of Economics* 9 (1978): 587–608. An introduction to "rational-choice Marxism" is John Roemer (ed.), *Analytical Marxism* (Cambridge University Press, 1986).

*Functional explanation in Marxism.* Good expositions of functional explanation are Robert Merton, *Social Theory and Social Structure* (Free Press, 1968), and Arthur Stinchcombe, *Constructing Social Theories* (Harcourt, Brace and World, 1968). The place of functional explanation in Marxist theory is discussed in G. A. Cohen, *Karl Marx's Theory of History* (Oxford University Press, 1978) and Philippe van Parijs, *Evolutionary Explanation in the Social Sciences* (Rowman and Littlefield, 1981). An account of some political implications of Marxist functionalism is Tang Tsou, "Back from the brink of revolutionary-'feudal' totalitarianism," in V. Nee and D. Mozingo (eds.), *State and Society in Contemporary China* (Cornell University Press, 1983), pp. 53–88, 268–75.

*Dialectics.* There are many good criticisms of the obscurantist aspects of dialectics, such as Karl Popper, "What is dialectics?" *Mind* 49 (1940): 403–26, or H. B. Acton, "Dialectical materialism," in P. Edwards (ed.), *The Encyclopedia of Philosophy* (Macmillan, 1968), 2: 389–97. I do not know of any exposition of the "rational core" of dialectics that makes it appear both plausible and nontrivial. The interpretation sketched here is further elaborated in my *Logic and Society* (Wiley, 1978).

# 3

# ALIENATION

M ARX found three main flaws in capitalism: inefficiency, exploitation, and alienation. These play two distinct roles in his theory. On the one hand, they enter into his normative assessment of what is wrong with capitalism and, as the other side of that coin, what is desirable about communism. On the other hand, they are part of his explanation of the breakdown of capitalism and the subsequent transition to communism. Clearly, the two roles are related. By and large, the various reasons why capitalism ought to be abolished also explain why it will be abolished. They receive, however, somewhat different emphases in the different parts of Marx's theory. The general theory of modes of production assigns the most important role to inefficiency in explaining why one mode is replaced by another. The theory of class struggle accords the central place to exploitation. The relation between these two explanatory theories will concern us later. In the normative theory, alienation is the most important concept. Marx valued communism above all because it would abolish alienation, in several senses of that term.

Does alienation play a role in the explanation of the breakdown of capitalism? It is not clear that it does, or that it can do. Alienation can be described, very broadly, as the lack of a sense of meaning. As such, it does not imply the sense of a lack of meaning. Only the latter, however, could provide a motivation for action. Consider the lack of self-realization, one of the main forms of alienation. If it takes the form of an unsatisfied desire for self-realization, it could motivate people to create a society in which the desire could be satisfied, assuming that they believe such a society to be feasible. If, however, people do not even have the desire, the fact that it could be satisfied in an alternative social organization has no explanatory power.

Neo-Marxists of the Frankfurt School have argued that the worst aspect of capitalism is that people do not even know that they are alienated. When they indulge in passive mass consumption instead of actively striving for individual self-realization, it is not because opportunities for the latter are lacking; it is because they have no desire for it. This paternalist, elitist, and pessimistic view was not held by Marx, at least not in the mature economic writings. There he praised capitalism for creating rich needs that it cannot satisfy, drawing a contrast between precapitalist societies in which men felt relatively content within a small circle of desires and the capitalist mode of production that multiplies desires beyond the creation of means to satisfy them. These desires, however, cannot influence the course of history before a new social mode that can satisfy them (on a mass scale) has become objectively possible, as a result of the development of the productive forces. Before that point, they are doomed to remain utopian. To summarize:

|  | Actual needs | Satisfied needs | Satisfiable needs |
|---|---|---|---|
| *Adaptive preferences* | small | small | small |
| *Subjective alienation* | large | small | large |
| *Objective alienation* | small | small | large |
| *Utopian preferences* | large | small | small |
| *Communism* | large | large | large |

Marx's concept of alienation, although of Hegelian origin, does not mean quite the same thing as Hegel's. In Hegel, alienation is the "negation" that mediates between primitive unity and differentiated unity in the history of mankind; it is a lack of unity and social integration. As such, it is a feature of Man, not of individual men. Marx located the phenomenon of alienation in a similar historical stage but at the level of individuals. This difference is related to the difference between Marx's ethical individualism and Hegel's ethical holism. Consistently with his methodological holism, Hegel believed that the creation of an organic community was a value in itself, over and above what valuable consequences it might have for individual men. Marx, on the other hand, took opposed stances on the methodological and ethical issues.

## ALIENATION: LACK OF SELF-REALIZATION

Marx believed that the good life for the individual was one of active self-realization. Capitalism offers this opportunity to a few but denies it to the vast majority. Under communism each and every individual will live a rich and active life. Although it will be closely bound up with the life of the community, it will be a life of *self*-realization.

Self-realization, for Marx, can be defined as the full and free actualization and externalization of the powers and abilities of the individual. Consider first the fullness of self-realization. It was one of Marx's more utopian ideas that under communism there will be no more specialized occupations. There will be no more painters, only people who among other things also paint. In a phrase from *The German Ideology* that has perhaps been taken more seriously than it was intended, people will hunt in the morning, fish in the afternoon, rear cattle in the evening, and be critical critics after dinner. The point is not simply that Marx neglects the need to choose between being a jack of all trades and a master of (at most) one. More importantly, this way of implementing the ideal of self-realization would defeat itself, because it would not allow one to benefit from the increasing marginal utility that is a major reason for preferring this mode of activity over consumption. This point is explained more fully later.

Even though self-realization cannot be full, it must be free. The ideal of self-realization is not compatible with society's coercing people to develop socially valuable talents at the expense of those they want to develop. The reason is that the "self" enters twice into the notion of self-realization, first as the designer and then as the raw material of the process. The person is endowed, on the one hand, with certain natural talents and capacities and, on the other hand, with a desire to develop some of them rather than others. The motivation behind self-realization derives from this peculiarly intimate relation.

The freedom of self-realization cannot imply that a good society will guarantee people the right to develop their preferred talents. If many people used this right to choose forms of self-realization that are very demanding of material resources, without a corresponding number choosing to realize themselves in ways that contribute to the creation of resources, the social account would not balance. True, Marx may be read as saying that communist society will be in a state of absolute abundance, with no material scarcity to constrain self-realization. On this interpretation, the freedom of self-realization would be as utopian as the fullness. A more charitable reading suggests, however, the weaker notion of freedom as lack of coercion. People might have to choose second-best or third-best lines of self-realization if they cannot find the material resources for their preferred option, but it would still be *their* choice, not someone else's.

Consider now the notion of self-realization itself. Corresponding to its two sources in Aristotle and Hegel, it may be decomposed into self-actualization and self-externalization. Self-actualization involves a two-step process of transforming a potential into actuality. The first step is the development of a potential ability into an actual one; the second is the deployment of the ability. A person who knows no French has the potential to speak French, at two removes from actuality. The potential of a person who knows French perfectly but is currently conversing in English is only one step removed. Self-externalization is the process whereby the powers of the individual become observable to other people. By acting and speaking in the presence of others, the person makes the self part of the public domain, with the risks and benefits that implies. The risk is that the self-image may be destroyed if it is not confirmed by others; the benefit, that it may achieve substance and solidity if it is so confirmed. In Freudian language, self-externalization involves the transition from the Pleasure Principle to the Reality Principle. Note that there can be self-actualization without self-externalization. The development of the ability to appreciate music or wine is an example.

There are two complementary questions we need to ask about the ideal of self-realization. First, what are its attractions compared to that of other life styles? Second, given those attractions, why is it not more frequently chosen over the alternatives? When suggesting answers to these questions I shall only compare self-realization and consumption, although these do not exhaust all the possibilities. Some people devote their lives to friendship or to contemplation. Because Marx does not consider these options, one might object that his is an impoverished view of human nature. One may reply on his behalf that only consumption and self-realization are proper objects of political philosophy, because unlike the other activities they compete for scarce material resources.

Two reasons for valuing self-realization derive from the two elements into which it was decomposed. Compare playing the piano with eating lamb chops. The first time one practices the piano it is difficult, even painfully so. By contrast, most people enjoy lamb chops the first time they eat them. Over time, however, these patterns are reversed. Playing the piano becomes increasingly more rewarding, whereas the taste for lamb chops becomes satiated and jaded with repeated, frequent consumption. Activities of self-realization are subject to increasing marginal utility: They become more enjoyable the more one has already engaged in them. Exactly the opposite is true of consumption. To derive sustained pleasure from consumption, diversity is essential. Diversity, on the other hand, is an obstacle to successful self-realization, as it prevents one from getting into the later and more rewarding stages. Because diversity also tends to be more expensive, this difference gives one reason for preferring self-realization over consumption.

The preceding argument appealed to the properties of self-actualization. Another argument derives from self-externalization. Doing something that is esteemed by other people is the most important source of self-esteem. Self-esteem, in turn, is what provides us with the motivation for going on with the business of living. Although not in itself a source of happiness, it is the basic condition for deriving happiness and satisfaction from other sources. Consumption, to be valuable, presupposes something that is not consumption.

Self-esteem can also be derived from self-externalization without self-actualization – from doing or producing something that others esteem sufficiently to pay for it, even if the work itself is monotonous and boring. What about the converse possibility? Self-actualization that remains inner and mute does not provide a durable satisfaction. The pleasures of self-actualization come not simply from using one's powers but from using them well. The evaluation must be performed by external observers according to independent, public criteria; otherwise one would sink into a morass of subjectivity, never knowing for sure whether one's achievements are real or spurious.

If self-realization really has these advantages, why is it not more frequently chosen? The answer could be the lack of opportunity, the lack of desire, or both. It is not easy in any industrial society to organize production in a way that combines efficiency with opportunities for individual self-realization. Neither assembly line work nor supervision of control screens is particularly rewarding in itself. Marx's models of self-realization are the artist, the scientist, or the preindustrial artisan, not the industrial worker. Although he always insisted that there was no turning back from industrial production, he did not really explain how there could be room for creative work in the modern factory, except for some remarks about the increasing importance of science in production.

We need to distinguish, however, between the obstacles to self-realization that stem from the nature of industrial production and those that derive from the capitalist organization of industry. In a socialist society the opportunities for self-realization might be multiplied. The state could encourage innovations that would facilitate efficient small-scale production. Individual firms, if owned and operated by the workers, could decide to organize production along lines more conducive to self-realization. Economic democracy itself could provide an outlet for self-realization, through participation in the decision-making processes of the firm.

Such reforms, however, presuppose a widespread desire for self-realization. If we look at contemporary Western societies, it is far from obvious that they would have much support. To some extent the lack of desire for self-realization may be explained by the lack of opportunities. People often end up not wanting what they cannot get, as in the fable of the fox and the grapes. There are, however, more specific reasons for the resistance to the ideal of self-realization. They can be summed up, briefly, as myopia, risk aversion, and free riding.

Myopia is the tendency to prefer present welfare over future welfare, just because it is present. A myopic person has difficulties in carrying out plans with the pattern "One step backward, two steps forward," because he or she will be deterred by the short-term sacrifice required. This, however, is exactly the pattern of self-realization. It requires a measure of self-control, of willingness to endure the less rewarding stages of self-actualization.

It also requires some willingness to take risks. A feature of self-realization not mentioned so far is that it is surrounded by uncertainty. It is difficult to know in advance exactly what gifts and talents one has. A given line of activity could turn out to be too easy and lead to boredom or too difficult and lead to frustration. For most people, frustration — trying and failing — is probably worse than boredom — succeeding too easily. If they are risk-averse, they will tend to choose the less ambitious vehicle for self-realization, which implies that on the average there will be less of it.

Self-realization, if successful, benefits the individual engaging in it. It may also, however, benefit others, if the chosen vehicle is technical, scientific, or artistic innovation. This points to a possible free-rider problem. It might be better for all risk-averse individuals if all behaved as if they were risk takers, because there would then be more innovation from which they could all benefit. Yet each individual would find it even better to be a free rider, benefiting from the risk-taking efforts of others while playing it safe for himself.

The combination of myopia, risk aversion, and free riding is a powerful force working against self-realization. Indeed, it works against it in two ways. In a society where there existed opportunities for self-realization, these attitudes would create the difficulties that I have described. People might believe that self-realization, abstractly speaking, is a good thing and yet not feel personally motivated to engage in it. Moreover, the same attitudes would stand in the way for a reform movement to create a society with more opportunities. The individual benefits of any large-scale reform process are remote in time, surrounded by uncertainty, and not dependent on individual participation. People might believe that socialism, abstractly speaking, is a good thing and yet not feel any personal motivation to bring it about. To overcome these obstacles, farsightedness and solidarity would be needed.

Alienation, in the present sense of the term, may be understood in several ways. It could simply mean the absence of self-realization. It could mean the absence of opportunities for self-realization, with or without the desire for self-realization. It could mean the presence of an ineffective desire for self-realization – that is, a desire blocked by myopia, risk aversion, or free riding – with or without opportunities for self-realization. Marx placed almost exclusive emphasis on the lack of opportunities for self-realization in capitalism. He also emphasized, however, that capitalism creates the material basis for another society in which the full and free self-realization of each and every individual becomes possible. Communism arises when this basis has been created. It is not clear whether he thought communism would arise when *and because* this basis has been created and, if he did, how the desire to overcome alienation is related to his other explanations of the breakdown of capitalism.

Is the value of self-realization compatible with that of community? Are they not rather on a course of head-on collision? Marx was very concerned with this issue. He wanted to distinguish communism from what Hegel had called "the spiritual animal kingdom" – a society of rampantly individualistic, competitive persons striving for their own personal self-realization at the expense of everything and everybody else. Of the several ways in which self-realization and community can be reconciled, he stressed one: self-realization for others. The bond of community arises from the knowledge that other people appreciate the activity or the product that is the vehicle of my self-realization, and that I similarly enjoy the external manifestation of their self-realization. This is not a reference to the community of creator-observers, which is implicit in the concept of self-externalization and is presupposed even in the most competitive forms of self-realization. It is a community of consumer-producers.

This reconciliation might be feasible in the small face-to-face communities of the past in which each producer knew his customers personally. Industrial societies, however, are depersonalized in two ways that combine to render it implausible. The social nature of production makes it impossible for any individual to point to any product as *his;* also, production for a mass market breaks the personal bond between producer and consumer. The idea that a person can have a feeling of community by knowing that he produces for "society" has no root in individual psychology.

A more plausible way of reconciling the two values is through production with others, or joint self-realization. Examples could be a small fishing vessel, a football team, a symphony orchestra, or decision making in direct economic democracy. In such interactions, we see the point of a remark in the *Communist Manifesto:* The free development of each becomes the condition for the free development of all. Again, it is not clear that industrial production lends itself easily to this synthesis. The historical trend seems to suggest that integrated work processes and self-realization in work are competing goals rather than complementary. The assembly line achieves a maximum of integration with a minimum of self-realization. Again, however, this might be due to the capitalist organization of industry rather than to the nature of industrial work.

### ALIENATION: LACK OF AUTONOMY

Social action may be understood at many levels. The immediate appearance is that people act freely and rationally to promote their ends, whatever these might be. Capitalism, in particular, has expanded the realm of freedom by making the scope for choice much greater than in any earlier form of society. Marx did not deny that freedom of choice in this sense is valuable. He added, however, that under capitalism it is twisted and subverted, at both ends, as it were. On the one hand, the formation of the desires occurs through a process the individual does not understand and with which he does not identify. Often, his own desires appear to him as alien powers, not as freely chosen. On the other hand the realization of the desires is often frustrated by lack of coordination and common planning. The aggregate outcome of individual actions appears as an independent and even hostile power, not as freely and jointly willed. The individuals are caught in the middle: between unintelligible psychological forces that shape their desires and equally opaque social forces that thwart them. The thin slice of freedom left after the operation of these forces now appears much less valuable.

Conversely, communism will do away with all processes operating "behind the back" of the individuals. Individuals will finally be autonomous – in full control not only over their actions but over the causes and the consequences of those actions. Individual psychology and social causality will become fully transparent. With respect to the economic study of capitalism, Marx wrote that all science would be superfluous if the essence of things coincided immediately with their appearance. In communism this coincidence will indeed obtain and will do away with the need for a social science.

Consider first the psychological, "subintentional," causal forces that operate behind the back of the individual. Although one cannot really say that Marx had a psychological theory, there are some remarks, notably in *The German Ideology*, that can be taken as a starting point for reflection. He suggests that in capitalism the desires of the individual are flawed in two ways: They tend to be one-sided as well as compulsive. The complaint about one-sidedness derives from the ideal of full self-realization, which I discussed and dismissed as utopian. It is also somewhat inconsistent with what Marx says about some of the great achievements in the past. He writes that Milton wrote *Paradise Lost* as a silkworm spins silk: because it was an activity of *his* nature. This is surely a more plausible view than that Milton could have taken time off, while writing *Paradise Lost*, to develop and deploy other talents.

This example also shows that there need not be anything objectionable about compulsive desires, if understood as desires so strong that they overwhelm all others. One may, however, justly object to compulsive desires if understood as desires with which the individual does not identify and which lead him to act in ways he does not understand and that give him no pleasure. Marx suggests that in capitalism the desire for consumption – as opposed to the desire for self-realization – tends to take on a compulsive character. Capitalism creates an incentive for producers to seduce consumers, by inducing in them new desires to which they then become enslaved. The desire for consumption goods creates a desire for the money that buys goods. This desire, though initially a derived one, takes on an independent existence in the compulsive desire to hoard precious metals; compulsive consumption gives way to the compulsive postponement of consumption characteristic of the miser. The perversion of human nature reaches its summit in the thirst for money for its own sake.

This analysis, though valuable and influential, has its limitations. It is not true that all or even most consumption in capitalist societies is compulsive. Without denying the importance of conspicuous consumption, "keeping up with the neighbors," and insidious techniques of consumer persuasion, I believe that most consumption satisfies needs that no one need be ashamed of having and, moreover, satisfies them in a perfectly respectable way. Conversely, compulsive desires for consumption goods will to some extent exist also in communism, or indeed in any society, because of the inherent addictiveness of many forms of consumption. Although the marginal utility of consumption is usually decreasing, the marginal disutility of not consuming – the strength of the withdrawal symptoms – may increase. Even if consumption were to be replaced by self-realization as the dominant value, there would still remain a good deal of consumption to which this argument would apply.

In any case, Marx's psychology is too simple. The distinction between compulsion and autonomy does not do justice to the complexities of human motivation. A stylized Freudian view appears more plausible. On this account, the autonomy of the person is threatened from two sides: by the tendency toward excessively impulsive or myopic behavior that Freud referred to as the Id and by the tendency toward rigid and compulsive behavior that he called the Superego. We may add, moreover, that the compulsiveness often arises because we are too successful in our strategies for coping with impulsive behavior: We become so afraid of yielding to pleasurable temptations that we lose all capacity for experiencing pleasure. The desirable balance, in which both threats are kept in abeyance, requires what is variously referred to as autonomy, ego strength, and toleration of ambiguity.

These problems derive from deep biological facts about human beings. They are not caused by capitalism, nor will they disappear with communism. This is not to say that the extent of the problems and the ability to deal with them are independent of historical context. The Victorians erred in their strong emphasis on self-control; other societies have erred in the opposite direction. Nevertheless, the desirable balance is fragile and vulnerable, too unstable to be achieved by all of the people all of the time.

The social or "supraintentional" causality that frustrates our desires has already been discussed. Some additional points can be made, however. We need to distinguish more clearly than Marx did between lack of transparence and lack of control. Consider first a case where the lack of control stems from the opacity of social causality and where, as the other face of the coin, insight suffices for control. Hog producers used to have a frustrating experience: Whenever they expected hog prices to be high and acted on that expectation, the opposite turned out to be the case. Conversely, when they expected low prices they got very good ones. One natural response could be to blame this on the weather, the government, or other external circumstances. In reality, however, the farmers were caught in a web of their own making. The expectations of high prices led them to produce more hogs than usual, which of course drove prices down; the expectation of low prices was self-undermining in the same way. Once the causality was clearly understood, and known to be understood, the cyclical fluctuations were eliminated. A self-fulfilling set of expectations emerged, stabilizing both prices and production.

In Keynesian wage cutting, however, insight does not improve the situation. In that case, as in any Prisoner's Dilemma, the strategy that leads to the collectively undesirable outcome has compelling individual rationality. Whether or not other firms cut wages, wage cutting is best for the individual firm. Understanding that other firms also cut wages and that together they make the situation worse for themselves than if they had all refrained from wage cutting makes no difference to the firm's behavior. The situation, although fully transparent, is out of control. To get it in hand, concerted action would be needed. This is exactly Marx's point: Only by coordinating their choices according to a common plan can people achieve freedom with respect not only to action but to the consequences of action. Otherwise, they are condemned in perpetuity to playing the sorcerer's apprentice.

Such collective lack of control is not unique to capitalism. Any market economy will be vulnerable to similar paradoxes of decentralized decision making. In particular, this holds for "market socialism," in which firms owned by the workers trade with each other in the market. Marx was very skeptical toward systems of this kind. His indictment of capitalism rested as much on the alienation created by horizontal division between firms and individuals as on the exploitation created by vertical division within firms. It is not just that market economies are unstable and their causality opaque. Even more importantly, in his eyes, markets operate by arm's-length transactions that subvert communitarian values and make people into mere means to one another's satisfaction. In *The German Ideology* Marx refers to this as "mutual exploitation." (This notion of exploitation differs from that of *Capital,* in which exploitation is necessarily asymmetrical.)

Yet any such indictment is incomplete as long as we are not told what the alternatives are. Today we know that central planning, which was the alternative Marx offered, has paradoxes that more than match those of the market system. Planning agencies are not monolithic units that make decisions and execute them as one single agent but complex social systems. The planning agents tend to undermine the plan by pursuing their own personal or bureaucratic interests. And even if their goals coincided perfectly with the common interest, their efforts would be frustrated by the enormous problem of gathering the information required for efficient planning. With respect to transparence and control, a centrally planned economy fares even worse than a market economy. A mixed economy, however, is superior to either pure form. On the one hand, market economies – capitalist or socialist – can to some extent be stabilized by macroeconomic planning; on the other hand, the state can provide certain public goods that the market fails to offer because it is not in the interest of any individual producer to do so. The "mutual exploitation" part of the indictment is undercut by the fact that any complex economy must be anonymous and depersonalized to a very large extent. In this respect central planning fares no worse and no better than reliance on markets.

These conclusions match that of the earlier discussion of self-realization. Marx concluded too rapidly that all the ills he observed in capitalism were due to capitalism. In reality, some of them are due to the nature of industrial work, others to biological facts about human beings, still others to problems inherent in coordinating complex activities. One utopian strand in his thinking was the overestimation of the degree to which each of the various evils of capitalism could be overcome. Another was his refusal to consider the possibility that it might not be possible to overcome all of them simultaneously to the degree that each of them could be overcome separately. The belief that all good things go together and the refusal to consider trade-offs between values are characteristic of utopian thinking.

Marx, nevertheless, prided himself that his socialism was scientific, not utopian. In this he was not totally wrong. Unlike many of his predecessors, he emphasized that communism could not arise until capitalism itself had created the requisite material conditions. Pure will was not sufficient to bring it about. Yet in spite of his realism with respect to the historical conditions for communism, his conception of that system itself was massively utopian. This fact detracts from his achievement; it does not destroy it. Stated with more realism and more sensitivity to the need for making hard choices, the ideals of self-realization and autonomy remain supremely valuable.

## ALIENATION: THE RULE OF CAPITAL OVER LABOR

In any productive process, Marx argued, all factors of production ultimately resolve into labor. He distinguished between living labor and dead labor – the first being the labor expended by workers during the production process, the second the labor embodied in the means of production. The produced means of production thus form a link between past, present, and future generations of workers. A mechanic in a machine tool shop works with machines produced by earlier workers to produce tools to be used by later workers.

These features of industrial work are perverted and distorted in capitalism. Here, the dead labor that is present alongside living labor in the production process appears as an alien and hostile power — as capital. Marx distinguishes between two stages in capital's domination of labor. In the first stage there is a merely "formal subsumption" of labor under capital. The capitalist exploits the worker through his ownership of the means of production but does not extend his domination to the process of production. This stage can be observed in the "putting-out" system of early capitalism. Here a capitalist provided a worker with raw materials and paid him a wage to transform them into a finished product — wool into cloth, for instance. In the second stage, the "real subsumption" of labor under capital, the capitalist moves into the process of production itself. This development culminates in factory production, in which the worker is reduced to an appendage of the machinery. Although in the first stage he had considerable freedom of movement, he must now work in step with the machines, under close, coercive supervision.

In both stages the worker is exploited by capital. By virtue of his ownership of capital, the capitalist can appropriate part of what the worker has produced. In the second stage there is an additional form of domination, in that the worker loses all autonomy and personal satisfaction from work. Capital is now more than a claim on surplus; it has become a tangible force that drains the worker of all energy and cripples all his talents. In Hegelian terminology, Objective Spirit dominates Subjective Spirit; in Marxist language, dead labor dominates living labor.

The irony and tragedy, for Marx, is that labor becomes the means to its own enslavement. The capital goods are products of human labor, which in turn come to dominate it. The root of this idea is the critique of religion that he took over from Ludwig Feuerbach. Marx assimilated the rule of dead labor to the religious fiction that represents men as created by a divine being whom, in reality, they have themselves created. Although these phenomena have a family resemblance to the theme of the sorcerer's apprentice, they go beyond it in an important respect. If I fail to control the consequences of my actions, I need not be or believe myself to be under anyone else's control. Being helpless and frustrated is not the same as being dominated. In particular, alienation-as-frustration, unlike alienation-as-subjection, is a fate that can be shared by everybody.

Alienation-as-subjection, though closely linked to exploitation, is not equivalent to it. Alienation adds to exploitation a belief on the part of the workers that the capitalist has a legitimate claim on the surplus, by virtue of his legitimate ownership of the means of production. The ownership, in turn, is seen as legitimate because derived from a legitimate appropriation of surplus at some earlier time. The efficacy of capitalist exploitation rests on its ability to perpetuate the conditions under which it appears as morally legitimate. Marx tells us that the recognition by labor of the products as its own and the judgment that the separation of labor from the products is unjust are the beginning of the end of capitalism. Alienation in this sense does not offer the workers a motivation to abolish capitalism; on the contrary, it blunts any such motivation.

FETISHISM

The capitalist economy secretes illusions about itself. There is the illusion that workers are free to escape exploitation, the illusion that capitalists are entitled to their ownership of the means of production, and the illusion that commodities, money, and capital have properties and powers of their own. The last Marx refers to as fetishism, with a reference to the religions that endow inanimate objects with supernatural powers. Economic fetishism begins as spontaneously arising illusions of everyday economic life and then solidifies into economic doctrine. Economists codify the natural illusions of the economic agents.

There are two ways of ascribing properties to objects. Both have the same surface grammatical form: $A$ is $F$. The book is red, the man is tall, the woman is rich. They differ, however, at a deeper level. The height of a person is a quality that inheres in him quite independently of social context. Wealth, on the other hand, can only be predicated of a person who is inserted in a web of social relations. It makes sense to say that Robinson Crusoe on his island was tall, not that he was rich, even if perhaps he brought some gold coins along with him. To be rich means that other people are willing to exchange their goods or labor for your money. Being rich, unlike being tall, is a relational predicate.

Economic fetishism, generally speaking, is the tendency to neglect the hidden or implicit relational structure of economic predicates. There are several kinds of fetishism, corresponding to different economic categories. Commodity fetishism is the belief that goods possess value just as they have weight, as an inherent property. To the unmystified mind, it is clear that a commodity has exchange value only because it stands in certain relations to human labor and human needs. In the bewitched world of commodity fetishism, however, goods appear to exchange at a certain rate because of their inherent values. Such, at any rate, was Marx's argument. It is somewhat unconvincing, because it is hard to believe that anyone ever committed this particular fallacy.

In other cases Marx's accusation of fetishism is more to the point. Money fetishism, in particular, is amply documented in history. This is the belief that money, especially in the form of precious metals, is inherently productive — not just a symbol of wealth but real wealth in its own right. The mercantilists and cameralists of the seventeenth and early eighteenth centuries were obsessed with the accumulation of precious metals. They believed, for instance, that a war could never be lost as long as gold and silver remained in the country — as if the metals could serve as food for soldiers and ammunition for guns. Even today, the monetary veil is often difficult to transpierce. Money fetishism is at work when trade unions define their goals in terms of nominal wages, independently of their purchasing power. The real economy is subject to hard constraints, but the monetary economy easily creates an illusion that it is possible to get something for nothing. In real terms a situation may be like a Prisoner's Dilemma in which everyone loses, but in monetary terms they may be able to deceive themselves into thinking they have gained.

Capital fetishism is the belief that capital's power to produce is a faculty inherent in it, not one it owes to the labor process. Both workers and capitalists are liable to this error. When a capitalist brings many workers together and their productivity increases more than proportionately to the number of workers, it appears to them, Marx argued, as if the extra productive power is due to capital. The capitalist falls into a similar illusion when facing the choice between investing his capital in production and depositing it in a bank to draw interest on it. Because from his point of view these actions are equally profitable, it is easy for him to think that they are equally productive. To dispel the illusion, it suffices to go through the thought experiment of imagining what would happen if all capitalists simultaneously took the second option.

The fetishism of interest-bearing capital and the closely related money fetishism correspond to widespread illusions about the relation between real and monetary accounting. The other forms of fetishism are less important. In particular, it is difficult to see why commodity fetishism has received so much attention, unless it is because it has been confused with other market-related phenomena. Commodity fetishism does not refer to the fact that one turns into a commodity something that ought not to be a marketable object, as in commercialized art or prostitution. Nor is it synonymous with "mutual exploitation" in market transactions. It is a cognitive illusion arising from market transactions, not a morally deplorable feature of markets.

BIBLIOGRAPHY

*Self-realization.* A thoughtful discussion of this aspect of alienation is John Plamenatz, *Karl Marx's Philosophy of Man* (Oxford University Press, 1975). The comparison between the temporal structure of self-realization and consumption draws on Richard Solomon and John Corbit, "An opponent-process theory of motivation," *Psychological Review* 81 (1974): 119–45. Useful discussions of self-realization through work are E. A. Locke, "Nature and causes of job satisfaction," in M. D. Dunnette (ed.), *Handbook of Industrial and Organizational Psychology* (Rand McNally College Publishing Co., 1976), pp. 1297–1349; J. R. Hackman, "Improving work design," in J. R. Hackman and J. L. Suttle (eds.), *Improving Life at Work* (Goodyear, 1977), pp. 96–162; G. E. O'Brien, "The centrality of skill-utilization for job design," in K. D. Duncan, M. M. Gruneberg, and D. Wells (eds.), *Changes in Working Life* (Wiley, 1980), pp. 167–87.

*Autonomy.* For an analysis of Marx's view that social causality in communism will be perfectly transparent, see G. A. Cohen, *Karl Marx's Theory of History* (Oxford University Press, 1978), app. 2. For some reasons why this view is implausible, see Raymond Boudon, *The Unintended Conse-*

*quences of Social Action* (St. Martin's Press, 1979). An economist's critique of consumer society is Tibor Scitovsky, *The Joyless Economy* (Oxford University Press, 1976). The best philosophical analysis is Raymond Geuss, *The Idea of a Critical Theory* (Cambridge University Press, 1981). The stylized Freudian theory is fully developed in George Ainslie, "A behavioral economic approach to the defence mechanism," *Social Science Information* 21 (1982): 735–80.

*The rule of capital over labor.* A good account of the self-perpetuating nature of exploitation is D. M. Nuti, "Capitalism, socialism, and steady growth," *Economic Journal* 80 (1970): 32–57.

*Fetishism.* The best account is chapter 5 in Cohen, *Marx's Theory of History.*

# 4

# MARXIAN ECONOMICS

## INTRODUCTION

CAPITAL I was published in 1867. That date marks the end of classical economics. It is generally agreed that modern economics was born around 1870, with the almost simultaneous achievements of Jevons in England, Walras in Switzerland, and Menger in Austria. Political bias apart, Marx's economic theory fell on deaf ears because it came at the wrong time. After his death it kept on a separate existence, interacting little with the mainstream of economic thought and undergoing little development. There were spurts of activity in the 1930s with the development of Keynesian Marxism, and then again in the 1960s with the successful Marxist refutation of a central part of neoclassical economics, as the mainstream has come to be called. These achievements did not, however, create a set of problems, theories, and concepts with a momentum of their own. Today Marxian economics is, with a few exceptions, intellectually dead. This, to be sure, is a subjective opinion. If one were to go by objective, quantitative facts, one would conclude that Marxian economics is flourishing. One observes all the normal signs of academic activity: specialized journals, "invisible colleges," appointments at major universities. Moreover, the technical rigor and mathematical sophistication of modern Marxian economics have done away with some of the obscurantism that used to reign unchallenged. It turns out, however, that it is possible to be obscurantist in a mathematically sophisticated way, if the techniques are applied to spurious problems.

The 1870 revolution introduced two closely related changes. First, it shifted the focus in economic theory from macroeconomic issues of growth and distribution toward microeconomic problems of economic decision making. Second, it introduced "marginalist" techniques, a branch of applied mathematics tailor-made for the study of rational choice. To get a flavor of the method, consider a typical economic problem: How many workers should a firm hire? The marginalist approach is to ask: How many workers does the firm have to hire before it becomes indifferent between hiring one extra worker and not hiring one? The argument assumes that all other factors of production (machinery, raw materials, etc.) are kept constant. Similar analyses may be carried out for each of these, enabling the firm to arrive at an overall decision of how much to buy of each factor.

On the one hand, an extra worker makes an addition to the total output of the firm. Typically, the additional output (the marginal product) decreases as the number of previously hired workers increases. The additional income to the firm may decrease even faster, if a higher output drives the price down. The firm will suffer from a reduced price on all the products it sells, not just on the products made by the newly hired worker. On the other hand, the firm has to consider the cost of hiring an extra worker. If the wage rate is given, it will hire workers up to the point where the extra net income created by one worker equals the wage. It could happen, however, that the demand for more workers drives the wage rate up; again, this will affect all workers, not just the last one to be hired. In that case the firm will hire workers up to the point where net income from an additional worker equals the total cost – his wage plus the wage increase he induces for all other workers – of hiring him.

This simple analysis rests on a number of presuppositions to which Marxists tend to take exception. First, there is the idea that each factor of production (labor in the example) has positive, although decreasing marginal productivity. Marx believed that production took place with "fixed coefficients," which means that the factors of production, to be productive, must be used in certain rigid proportions. If the factors are employed in these proportions, hiring an extra worker yields no extra output. Second, the analysis presupposes that the supply of workers can depend on the wage rate, that is, that workers are sometimes induced to work – or to work more – by higher wages. The Marxist view, on the contrary, is that workers are forced to sell their labor power. Third, it was presupposed that the firm, to sell all its products, must set the price lower the more it wants to sell. The price depends on how much the least interested customer is willing to pay. Marx, on the other hand, argued that price is determined by cost, not by demand.

Of these disagreements, the first can be definitely resolved: Marx was wrong. An extra worker does make it possible to use given machines and raw materials more efficiently. Keeping in mind that similar statements hold for the other factors of production, this creates much more scope for entrepreneurial deliberation and choice than Marx allowed. The other disagreements are more ambiguous. A Marxist could argue that in perfect competition the individual firm must take wages and prices for given; indeed, perfect competition is defined by the assumption that each firm is too small to affect factors and product prices. To this one may reply, first, that in the age of "monopoly capitalism" economics also needs to study imperfect competition and, second, that even in perfect competition the Marxist analysis is inadequate. Even assuming no relation at the firm level between the wage rate and the number of workers employed, the fact that there is such a relation at the national level conflicts with the view that workers are forced to sell their labor power. Similarly, even though an individual firm can take the price of its product as a given outcome of market forces, demand *is* an element of the latter and, as such, can affect prices.

The upshot of this discussion is that Marxian economics errs by exaggerating the importance of structural constraints and by minimizing the scope for rational choice. Workers and capitalists make decisions by comparing alternatives and choosing the one that best will promote their goals. Workers face the choice between more leisure and a higher income, a choice complicated by the fact that without money it may be difficult to fill the leisure time. The fact that this problem was unimportant in English capitalism around 1850 does not imply that it can justifiably be neglected in contemporary, more affluent capitalist societies. Capitalists must compare the effects – direct and indirect, positive and negative – of different combinations of factors of production. They must also consider which employee career structure is most profitable for the firm, how much to spend on advertising, and a number of other decision problems that hardly existed in Marx's time. Only by blatantly ignoring economic reality could one say that all these choices are foreordained by economic necessity.

Microeconomics is not all of economics, however. Although methodological individualism tells us that all economic theory ought ultimately to be rooted in the theory of individual economic decisions, there are many branches of economics in which this program is not yet practicable and in which the units of analysis are some kind of aggregate entities. Keynesian macroeconomics is a theory of aggregate saving, investment, and consumption whose microfoundations remain shaky. The neoclassical theory of distribution and growth turns on the relation among aggregate capital, aggregate labor, and aggregate output. Although Marxist economists have done an excellent job in showing that this theory fails because of lack of microfoundations, they have not been equally critical toward Keynesian macroeconomics. Indeed, current Marxian economics is almost as strongly influenced by Keynes as by Marx. A third branch of macroeconomics studies the physical balancing of the various industries or sectors in the economy by considering the forward and backward connections that obtain between them. This input–output analysis was pioneered by Marx. Although perhaps his most significant analytical accomplishment, this analysis of "economic reproduction" is also one of his less "Marxist" achievements. It is more like a bookkeeping account writ large than a study of economic causality.

## THE LABOR THEORY OF VALUE

One of the most fundamental questions of economics is how to explain the prices at which commodities exchange against each other. Empirical economics studies the prices that can be observed in actual markets. Theoretical economics studies the prices that arise in market equilibrium, when all agents – consumers and producers – have made the best choices they can at the ruling prices. Marxian price theory is an equilibrium theory. Although Marx certainly did not believe that capitalism was in or near equilibrium most of the time, he nevertheless found it an intellectual challenge to explain the prices that would obtain in equilibrium. Like most of the classical economists, Marx tried to explain price formation by a *labor theory of value*. The rates at which goods exchange against each other are explained by the amount of labor that has gone into their production.

The theory has a certain immediate appeal. If I spend six hours putting straws together to form a mat and you spend three hours to catch one fish from the stream with your hands, the expected rate of exchange − if there is an exchange − would be two fish against one mat. I would not be satisfied with anything less than two fish, because I could have caught that amount myself in the time I spent making the mat; similarly, you would not settle for less than the whole mat. Notice, however, the extreme simplifications in this story. Raw materials are assumed to be available freely and costlessly. Production is assumed to take place without the use of produced means of production. The two kinds of work are assumed to be equally irksome or unpleasant. Acquired skills are ignored, as are inborn talents. When we introduce the complications that the story assumed away, the labor theory of value becomes difficult to defend, or even to state coherently.

The most basic difficulty stems from the existence of inborn differences of skill. If you could have made my mat in five hours whereas I would have spent four hours catching one of your fish, simply because of inborn skill differences, it becomes difficult to predict how the goods will exchange. If there are just the two of us, we will bargain over the price, with an outcome that is in general difficult to predict, even if we add information about how strongly each of us desires the two goods. If we assume that there are one million people exactly like you and one million like me, competition between individuals will reduce the scope for bargaining, and we will be able to predict the equilibrium price. There is no way, however, in which we can explain the price by the relative amounts of labor that have been expended, because that ratio is not well defined. To use just labor time, without taking account of the qualitative difference between skilled and unskilled labor, would be as absurd as explaining the price difference between a sack of potatoes and a sack of rice by comparing their weights.

There is, moreover, no way in which one could define a conversion factor that would allow us to translate one hour of skilled labor into so many hours of unskilled labor. There is a way of doing this in the case of acquired skills: We simply look at the amount of labor that has gone into the production of the skill out of unskilled labor power. Inborn skills, however, are inherently noncomparable. True, one might compare them through the wages paid to workers with different skills, but this would go against Marx's view that in capitalism labor power is just one commodity among others, whose price is determined by the amount of labor that goes into its production. The wages of skilled workers reflect the demand for the goods they produce, whereas a main virtue of the labor theory of value is supposed to be its independence of demand conditions.

Just as workers may differ in their skill, work tasks may differ in being more or less pleasant. If you and I both find catching fish more irksome than making mats, the ensuing exchange rate would be different. If you like catching fish and I prefer making mats, this might or might not affect the exchange rate, depending on the strength of the feelings and on our ability to bluff and bargain. Again, nothing can be explained simply by comparing the number of hours spent on making the products, and there is no way of converting one form of labor into another. And again, comparing the tasks through a comparison of the wages they command would be contrary to Marx's intention, which was to provide an objective, materialist account of price formation that did not depend on subjective attitudes toward work.

These objections, if correct, show that the notion of *the* labor value of a good is not well defined. Let us, nevertheless, consider the prospect of the labor theory of value in a world in which they do not apply, a world in which all skill differences are acquired by training and all work tasks are equally onerous. In economic models – neoclassical no less than Marxist – abstractions of this magnitude are performed as a matter of routine. It is almost invariably assumed, for instance, that there are no economies of scale in production, in spite of the overwhelming importance of this phenomenon in the real world. The status and value of insights generated by such drastic simplifications are unclear, to put it charitably. If, however, we stick to the rules of the economic models game as it is currently played, a discussion of the labor theory of value under these simplifying assumptions is perfectly in order.

The labor theory of value says that the prices of goods are explained by their labor content. A particularly simple explanation, which was held by most classical economists before Marx, would be that prices are proportional to labor content. Marx, however, knew well that this was not true in general. To see why, we must introduce the basic notions of Marxian economics.

The *labor value* of a good is the sum total of the labor that, directly and indirectly, is needed to produce it. Equivalently, one may also think of labor value as an "employment multiplicator": It is the amount of labor that would have to be added to an economy in order to make it possible to produce one more unit of the good. Some of this extra labor would come in the industries that produce the good in question, some of it would come in the industries producing capital goods for the first set of industries, and so on throughout the whole economy. Another, equivalent way of thinking about the labor value is as the sum of a series of past labor inputs. Consider the production of grain, using only labor and seed grain as inputs, with seed grain yielding tenfold. The labor value of one ton of grain is the sum of the direct labor expended this year to produce it out of 100 kilo of seed grain, *plus* the labor expended last year to produce 100 kilo seed grain, *plus* the labor expended the year before last to produce the 10 kilo seed grain that produced those 100 kilo, and so on. This infinite series of ever smaller labor inputs adds up to a finite sum, which is the labor value of the ton of grain.

*Constant capital* is the labor value of nonlabor means of production: machinery, buildings, raw materials that have already been somewhat refined by labor. (To make things simpler, we imagine that all constant capital is used up in one production period.) *Variable capital* is the labor value of the labor power of the workers employed in the production process. In Marx's view, the labor power of the worker is a commodity like any other, not only in being bought and sold on the market but in being produced out of other commodities. The labor power of the worker is produced out of the goods he consumes; hence the labor value of his labor power is defined by the labor value of these goods, which he consumes in fixed proportions just as production takes place with fixed proportions of inputs. *Surplus value* is the difference between the value the worker produces in a given period and the value of the consumption goods needed to sustain him for that period. Let us refer to constant capital, variable capital, and surplus value in the economy as a whole as $C$, $V$, and $S$, respectively, and to the same magnitudes in one particular sector as $c$, $v$, and $s$.

We can then define three aggregate ratios that play an important part in Marxian economics. *The rate of exploitation* (also called the rate of surplus value) is the ratio $S/V$. *The organic composition of capital* (a rough measure of capital intensity) is the ratio $C/V$. *The rate of profit* is the ratio $S/(C + V)$. To see how these three ratios are related to each other, divide both the numerator and the denominator in the rate of profit by $V$. We obtain

$$\text{The rate of profit} = \frac{\text{the rate of exploitation}}{\text{the organic composition of capital} + 1}$$

This has some claim to be called *the fundamental equation of Marxian economics*. Marx believed, wrongly, that he could use the fundamental equation to derive the equilibrium rate of profit that must obtain in each and every sector of the economy. One can use it, however, to show that prices cannot be proportional to values.

Assume, namely, that this proportionality obtained. In that case the magnitudes $c$, $v$, $s$ could be interpreted as prices as well as values, and the fundamental equation would be correct with respect to any given industry. The surplus value would appear as profit; the sum of constant and variable capital would appear as cost; dividing through yields the rate of profit. Let us now compare two firms that produce in industries with different organic compositions of capital and assume that the rate of exploitation is the same in both. This last assumption is justified because competition in the labor market ensures that workers in the two firms work the same number of hours and reproduce their labor power with the same consumption goods. But if the firms operate with the same rate of exploitation and different organic compositions of capital, their profit rates must differ. This, however, cannot obtain in equilibrium. If some industries have higher profits than others, capital will flow from the low-profit sectors to the high-profit sectors until equality of profit is achieved. Because the hypothesis that equilibrium prices are proportional to values leads to the self-contradictory conclusion that firms will have different profit rates in equilibrium, the hypothesis must be false.

In order to deduce equilibrium prices from values, Marx proposed the following procedure. First, he used the fundamental equation to derive $r$, the equilibrium rate of profit. To deduce the price of any given good, he multiplied the labor value of the inputs used to produce it – the constant and the variable capital – by $(1 + r)$. Price, in other words, is derived by adding a markup on costs. This proposal is fundamentally flawed. For one thing, the reasoning can only be characterized as a dialectical howler; for another, it does not yield the correct results.

Marx believed that the relation between labor values and prices was an instance of Hegel's theory of the essence and the appearance. Prices appear on the surface, in the sense that unlike labor values they are immediately visible to the economic agents. To explain the relative prices, however, we must go beyond the surface to the deep structure of the economy – to labor values. An analogy could be the relation between the visible appearance of a physical object and the atomic structure that explains why it appears that way – as green rather than yellow, for example. This understanding of Hegel was probably incorrect, although the impenetrable density of Hegel's *Science of Logic* – where the distinction between essence and appearance is expounded – makes it hard to be sure. In any case, Marx's deduction of prices violates the idea that values are deep structural entities, hidden to the economic agents whose behavior they regulate. The deduction of prices by a markup on cost *as measured in labor values*, presupposes that the capitalists know what these values are – contrary to the view that they are hidden and invisible. It is as if, in a study of the physiology of perception, one stipulated that people must know a lot about atomic physics in order to have the visual impressions they have.

Here is how a correct deduction would go. The problem is to determine certain unknown quantities: the rate of profit and the set of relative prices. With, say, 15 goods, there are 14 relative prices, if the price of the last good is set equal to 1 by convention. Hence, in this case, there are 15 unknowns to be found. To find them, we need 15 equations. For each of the 15 goods we set up an equation stating that cost plus profit equals price. The cost is the sum of the prices of the inputs used to produce the good, where the inputs are given by the ''fixed coefficients'' of production and the similarly fixed coefficients of consumption. The profit is the cost multiplied by the rate of profit. Solving these 15 equations with 15 unknowns, we derive the rate of profit and the relative prices in one fell swoop, whereas Marx wrongly thought he could derive the rate of profit before he deduced prices. It is a useful exercise to set up a two-sector example to show that Marx's method does not give the same result as the correct procedure. Note that in the latter labor values play no role whatsoever. To deduce equilibrium prices and the rate of profit, we must know the technical coefficients, but there is no need to know the labor values. We may calculate them, if we want to, but once we have done so there is no further use to which they can be put.

A very problematic part of Marx's economic theory is the idea that labor power is produced with a fixed set of consumption goods rather than paid a monetary wage that the workers can proceed to spend as they please. This view confuses capitalism and slavery and conflicts with what Marx says elsewhere about the greater freedom of choice that distinguishes capitalism. He held this mechanistic conception because without it he could not define the notion of *the* value of labor power. If workers receive a monetary wage, they can spend it in many different ways, on many different baskets of consumption goods. Even though all of these add up to the same total price, they need not have the same total labor content. The latter conclusion would follow only if prices were in general proportional to labor values, a view that Marx rightly discarded.

## REPRODUCTION, ACCUMULATION, AND TECHNICAL CHANGE

A state of economic equilibrium has two properties. On the one hand, prices must be such that producers can cover their costs and earn the average profit. This is a condition that holds within each sector or industry. On the other hand, productive output in one period must be such as to yield the inputs necessary for production and consumption in the next period. This is a condition that holds between different sectors and determines their size relative to one another. We have seen that Marx's analysis of price equilibrium was irremediably flawed. His theory of physical equilibrium, however, though not faultless, was more valuable. The analyses in *Capital II* of simple and extended reproduction anticipated later theories of input–output analysis and of balanced multisectoral growth. Even more important and influential are the chapters in *Capital I* that propose a broad historical perspective on the rise and development of the capitalist mode of production.

Let us first consider the conditions under which the economy can reproduce itself identically, assuming that the whole surplus goes to capitalist consumption and that no reinvestment takes place. Following Marx, we divide the economy into two sectors. Sector I is the capital goods sector, whereas sector II produces consumption goods for workers and capitalists alike. The total value of the output produced in the two sectors can be decomposed into $c_I + v_I + s_I$ and $c_{II} + v_{II} + s_{II}$, respectively. Because we have assumed that constant capital is completely used up during the period of production, the output of sector I must in equilibrium be exactly equal to the constant capital employed in the two sectors: $c_I + v_I + s_I = c_I + c_{II}$. Also, the output of sector II must be exactly sufficient to cover working-class consumption (corresponding to the variable capital) and capitalist consumption (corresponding to the surplus): $c_{II} + v_{II} + s_{II} = v_I + s_I + v_{II} + s_{II}$. Both equations reduce to the same condition: $c_{II} = v_I + s_I$. Physical equilibrium for simple reproduction requires that the value of the constant capital used to produce consumption goods equal the value added in the capital goods sector.

Actual capitalist economies do not, however, conform to this pattern. What makes capitalism tick is not only that capitalists make a profit by exploiting workers but that they reinvest part of the profit in further production. "Accumulate, accumulate! That is Moses and the prophets!" Accumulation may be extensive or intensive. It may take the form of quantitative expansion without technical change or of investment in new technology that brings about a qualitative transformation of the production process.

It is not quite clear what, in Marx's view, was the relation between extensive and intensive accumulation. One account, with some basis in his work, is the following. The need to save and reinvest is the fundamental driving force in capitalism. Initially, investment takes the form of subjugating noncapitalist sectors of the economy to capitalist rule, as in the putting-out system of early capitalism. At the same time we observe the expansion, on a given technical basis, of sectors that have already been organized on a capitalist basis. Sooner or later, however, these purely quantitative forms of growth come up against their limits. Expansion into the noncapitalist environment comes to a halt when all sectors have come under the rule of capital. Expansion of the capitalist sectors comes up against the limited supply of labor, decreasing demand for the given range of products, or both. Capital is forced to channel its expansive tendencies into innovation and qualitative economic growth. This is the revolutionary phase of capitalism, and that which creates the basis for its own supersession.

The puzzle is why the reinvestment motive arose in the first place. What are the psychological or economic forces that would lead a capitalist to reinvest part of the surplus, instead of consuming all of it? Max Weber's answer, in *The Protestant Ethic and the Spirit of Capitalism,* was that saving and reinvestment were a solution to a psychological tension that inhabited the puritan or Calvinist entrepreneur. His religion told him that salvation was a matter of predestination: The elect had already been chosen from eternity on, and nothing he could do would affect his chances. He could, however, affect his belief that he was among the elect by engaging in behavior that could be seen as a sign that he was chosen. An eighteenth-century Methodist pamphlet illustrates this form of magical thinking when, having exhorted people to come to a religious meeting, it adds that "The coming soul need not fear that he is not elected, for none but such would be willing to come."

This argument was hardly open to Marx, because it would appear to give religious, nonmaterial forces an independent explanatory power that he was not willing to accord them. In some of his writings he offered a dialectical deduction of "the self-expansion of value," as if a real historical development could be explained by mere conceptual juggling. In others he suggested a more satisfactory account: Capitalists are forced to invest by competition. This argument, however, does not support the distinction between extensive and intensive accumulation. Competition forces the entrepreneur to invest in more efficient methods, so that he can undersell his competitors; it does not force him to expand in a merely quantitative manner. The history of capitalism does not divide into a stage of extensive growth followed by one of intensive growth. From the very beginning it was characterized by innovation and qualitative expansion. Quantitative expansion may be retained as an aspect of this process but not as a chronologically separate stage. Of these two accounts, the first has better basis in Marx's writings, whereas the second seems to correspond more closely to the actual historical development.

Merely quantitative expansion or, as Marx called it, extended reproduction also has its equilibrium conditions. The capital goods produced by sector I must cover the replacement of constant capital in both sectors *plus* the demand for new capital derived from the new investment. The consumption goods produced in sector II must cover the consumption of capitalists and workers in the expanded economy. We stipulate, furthermore, that capitalists in both sectors have similar saving behavior. In his numerical examples Marx did not respect the last condition, but in the absence of specific reasons for thinking otherwise it seems to be a reasonable one. Some followers of and commentators on Marx have spelled it out as a requirement that capitalists in both sectors save the same proportion of the surplus value created in their sectors. This, however, embodies the very same dialectical howler that Marx committed in his deduction of prices from values. Saving belongs to the realm of money and prices, not to the world of labor values. The proper equilibrium condition, therefore, must be that the same proportion of profits is saved in both sectors. Contrary to what Marx believed, the conditions for extended reproduction cannot be stated in labor-value accounting.

Technical change – the development of the productive forces – is at the heart of historical materialism. It is what explains the rise and fall of the successive modes of production. Capitalism, like any other mode of production based on exploitation and class divisions, is both a spur and a bridle on technical change. It becomes superseded when and because the bridle effect comes to dominate the spur effect – a statement that will be clarified later.

Capitalism acts as a spur on technical change by making innovation a question of survival for the firm. The dynamism of the capitalist mode of production comes from competition between firms in the market, not from the capital–labor relationship within the firm. That relationship, by contrast, is responsible for the bridles that capitalism imposes on innovation. According to Marx, the exploitation of labor by capital acts as a fetter on technical change, in two distinct ways.

First, the criterion by which a capitalist accepts or rejects new techniques is a socially undesirable one. In a rationally organized society, the criterion for choice of techniques is the minimization of labor time, because work even at its best is a form of drudgery that ought to be reduced as much as possible. (At least this is what Marx argued in *Capital*. In other writings he was more open to the idea that work under communism will be a value in itself, as a means to self-realization.) In capitalism, the criterion is the maximization of profit or the minimization of *paid* labor time. Hence, Marx argued, the scope for machinery would be greater under communism than under capitalism. There may be something to that argument but certainly less than Marx claimed. A rational planner would consider not only the sum of the series of labor inputs needed to produce the good but also the temporal profile of the series, a consideration that would bring him closer to the profit-maximizing criterion.

Second, Marx argued that the class struggle may prevent a capitalist owner from adopting the most efficient technique. An innovation that would increase the profit at a given wage rate may also lead to a wage increase that offsets the efficiency gain. Innovations are usually embodied in new machinery and physical plant. The physical organization and layout of the factory may in turn affect the class consciousness and combativity of the workers. The workers are disciplined, united, and organized by the very process of factory production: Capitalism produces its own gravediggers. A rational and foresighted capitalist would anticipate this effect and, if necessary, sacrifice a short-term increase of profit for the sake of long-term maintenance of power. The argument, though potentially important, is incomplete. Because the level of working-class consciousness is not determined by the technical choices of a single capitalist, there could easily arise a free-rider problem. All capitalists might be better off if they all refused to adopt a certain innovation, but the consequences for any one capitalist of adopting it might not suffice to deter him.

## CRISIS THEORY

In his relentless indictment of capitalism, Marx adopted both external and internal standards of criticism. On the one hand, he compared the actual level of want satisfaction and technical change with the level that would obtain in a communist society. This comparison underlies the central indictments produced by the theory of alienation and by historical materialism. On the other hand, he argued that capitalism fails to deliver the goods even in its own terms. In particular, it is prone to recurrent economic crises that undermine any claim to being a rational way of organizing production and distribution. This part of the case for the prosecution is argued in the three volumes of *Capital.*

Sometimes it seems that Marx made capitalism out to be more perversely irrational than it could possibly be. He appears to claim that it would lead both to ever greater impoverishment of the workers *and* to a fall in the rate of profit enjoyed by the capitalist class. Although capitalism produces a massive acceleration of the productive forces, no one would actually benefit from that development. On closer reading, however, Marx can be absolved from this implausible view. In the mature economic writings, which set out the theory of the falling rate of profit, there is no suggestion that the standard of living of the workers will fall in the literal sense. It might fall relative to that of the capitalist class, and relative to the level that would be achieved in a rationally planned society, but not in absolute terms.

An important crisis theory among pre-Marxist critics of capitalism was the disproportionality theory. It asserts that in an unplanned economy the conditions for simple or extended reproduction are unlikely to be met, except by accident. Because there is no coordinating agency to ensure that inputs to production will be available in the requisite proportions, we observe a perpetual combination of waste and shortage. All this, though true, is somewhat simplistic. As Marx well knew, excess supply of goods tends to lower prices and reduce supply; excess demand is eliminated by a similar self-regulating mechanism. Marx did not, however, take the further step and ask whether these reactions could overshoot and, instead of restoring equilibrium, create a deviation from it in the opposite direction. The "hog cycle" illustrates this case. This is a rare instance in which Marx credited capitalism with more collective rationality than it in fact possesses, because he did not fully grasp the dynamics of price adjustments.

Nor did he fully understand the dynamics of wage adjustments. There are many passages, notably in the *Grundrisse*, where Marx was tantalizingly close to the central insights of Keynesian economics. He was fully aware of the paradoxical character of a system in which each capitalist wants his workers, but only his workers, to be badly paid. He also entertained, albeit in a very vague form, the theory that crises are due to lack of purchasing power among the workers. The two ideas remained separate in his writings, however. It was left for Keynes to bring them together, in his analysis of the self-reinforcing process of falling demand and wage cuts.

The theory of the falling rate of profit was Marx's main account of the economic breakdown of capitalism. Like the other classical economists, Marx wanted to explain the secular tendency of the rate of profit to fall. The view of his predecessors was quite similar to that of modern environmentalist concerns. The combined effect of population growth and depletion of resources was to slow down economic development, with stagnation as the ultimate outcome. The main culprit was diminishing marginal productivity in agriculture: To produce food for more workers, land of lower quality had to be taken into use, leading to higher food prices, higher wages, and lower profits. Technical change might counteract and delay this tendency but only for a while.

Marx offered an explanation that differed in two respects. The cause of the falling rate of industrial profit had to be sought in industry itself, not in agriculture. Technical change, far from being a counteracting tendency to the falling rate of profit, was the very cause of the fall. The last claim sounds strange, and it is indeed quite indefensible. It has, nevertheless, a certain superficial plausibility, without which it could not have exerted such a strong attraction on generations of later Marxists. Indeed, at first glance it appears plausible on dialectical no less than on mathematical grounds, an apparently unbeatable combination.

A dialectical rendering of the argument is the following. Technical change tends to be labor-saving. When capitalists substitute dead labor for living labor, which is the ultimate source of all profit, they behave in a collectively self-destructive way. Each capitalist has an incentive to innovate, to gain a cutting edge in competition, but when all innovate all suffer. The capitalists face a Prisoner's Dilemma. An algebraic version of the argument is the following. The tendency of innovations to be labor-saving means, in Marx's language, that there is an increasing organic composition of capital. It then follows from the fundamental equation of Marxian economics that if the rate of exploitation is constant, the rate of profit must fall.

These, however, are treacherous formulations that cannot be upheld in a more rigorous treatment. Although the view that technical change is inherently labor-saving appears very plausible, especially in the day of the computer revolution, it is not borne out by the facts. It neglects such dramatic capital-saving innovations as explosives and the wireless. Historically, innovations have saved more or less equally on labor and on capital.

Even if we granted that there is a labor-saving bias on the whole, we could not conclude to an increase in the organic composition of capital. If one industry has a labor-saving innovation, it would indeed experience an increase in the organic composition, but if we assume – as Marx did – that such innovations occur across the board, in all industries, the link is broken. Innovations in the industry that produces capital goods for the industry in which a labor-saving innovation has occurred reduce the value of these goods and lower the organic composition of capital in the latter industry.

Finally, Marx did not consistently adhere to the assumption that the rate of exploitation remains constant. In the presence of technical process, this assumption implies that real wages are rising in absolute terms: There is no absolute impoverishment. It also implies that the shares of labor and capital of the net social product remain constant, so that there is no relative impoverishment either. Marx suggests that the actual development is one in which wages rise in absolute terms but fall in relative terms, so that there is an increase in the rate of exploitation. He gives no reasons for thinking, however, that the net effect of an increase in both the numerator and the denominator of the fundamental equation will be a fall in the rate of profit.

Marx's theory of the falling rate of profit leaks like a sieve. To understand how he could have held the extremely counterintuitive view that innovation causes a fall in the rate of profit, we may consider the following explanations. Although Marx – contrary to a widespread view – was not averse to the use of mathematics in economic analysis, he was not trained in it. It is difficult to carry out the kind of analysis he attempted without the technical tools for evaluating the net effect of complex social processes. Also, there may have been an element of wishful thinking at work. There is a pleasing paradox in the view that the driving force of capitalism – its relentless tendency to innovation – will also be the cause of its breakdown. Most importantly, perhaps, the argument for an increase in the organic composition of capital rested on a confusion between the qualitative and the quantitative domination of labor by capital. The qualitative domination is the real subsumption of labor under capital, whereby the worker is reduced to a mere cog in a gigantic machine. The quantitative domination is the increase in the organic composition. It is difficult to understand today how a mere numerical fraction can take on the significance of the domination of Objective Spirit over Subjective Spirit. For Marx, this Hegelian algebra was self-evidently true.

BIBLIOGRAPHY

*Introduction.* On the place of Marxian economics in the history of economic analysis, see Mark Blaug, *Economic Thought in Retrospect,* 3d ed. (Cambridge University Press, 1985). The Marxist critique of neoclassical growth theory is explained in G. C. Harcourt, *Some Cambridge Controversies in the Theory of Capital* (Cambridge University Press, 1973).

*The labor theory of value.* Excellent expositions, in increasing order of difficulty, are Ian Steedman, *Marx after Sraffa* (New Left Books, 1977), Michio Morishima, *Marx's Economics* (Cambridge University Press, 1973), and John Roemer, *Analytical Foundations of Marxian Economics* (Cambridge University Press, 1981). They may be usefully supplemented by C. C. von Weizsäcker, *Steady-State Capital Theory* (Springer, 1971), and by Ugo Pagano, *Work and Welfare in Economic Theory* (Blackwell, 1985).

*Reproduction, accumulation, and technical change.* Morishima's *Marx's Economics* is good on the first two topics, Roemer's *Analytical Foundations* is an outstanding exposition of the third. On the relation between competition and technical change in early capitalism, see especially Robert Brenner, "The agrarian roots of European capitalism," *Past and Present* 97 (1982): 16–113.

*Crisis theory.* On the falling rate of profit, see again Roemer, *Analytical Foundations,* and Philippe van Parijs, "The falling-rate-of-profit theory of crisis: a rational reconstruction by way of obituary," *Review of Radical Political Economy* 12 (1980): 1–16.

# 5

# EXPLOITATION

## INTRODUCTION

THE contrast and the conflict between the haves and the have-nots, the idle rich and the working poor, are constant themes of history. Marx's theory of exploitation is an attempt to provide a scientific, rigorous statement of these intuitive notions. In his work as a whole it serves two distinct purposes. On the one hand, it has an explanatory function. Exploitation, when perceived by the exploited, provides a motivation for revolt, protest, riot, or revolution. As such it can enter into the explanation of class struggle and social change. On the other hand, exploitation is a normative concept that is part of a wider theory of distributive justice. Exploitation, whether perceived by the exploited or not, is morally wrong. It is unfair that some should be able to earn an income without working or out of proportion with their work contribution.

The two purposes do not fully match. The normatively relevant concept of exploitation may not have strong motivational force. Because of a limited horizon, in space or time, the exploited may make mistakes about the identity of the exploiters and about the extent to which they are exploited. Workers may focus their struggle on managers, when in reality these are only passing on the surplus to shareholders. They may focus on the size of the surplus that is extracted from them, without noticing that part of it is reinvested in future production that partly redounds to their benefit. Exploitation, in the appropriate normative sense, is a highly abstract concept, whereas the class struggle is motivated by more immediate concerns.

Marx's notion of exploitation has a very specific content. A person is exploited, in Marx's sense, if he performs more labor than is necessary to produce the goods that he consumes. If he actually produces his own consumption goods, the criterion for exploitation is simply whether he also produces goods to be consumed by others. This was the case in feudalism, where the serfs worked some days on their own land and the rest of the week on the lord's land. In other modes of production the exploited perceive their situation in a different light. Slaves, Marx argued, tend to think that all their labor is unpaid labor, forgetting that part of it covers the cost of reproducing their labor power. Wage workers, by contrast, are easily misled into thinking that all their labor is paid labor, because they are actually paid by the hour. It is only in feudalism that the appearance of exploitation coincides with its essence – the performance of labor over and above what is needed to produce the goods consumed by the laborer.

Conversely, a person is an exploiter if he works fewer hours than are needed to sustain his consumption. For there to be exploiters, there must also be some who are exploited. Strictly speaking, the converse need not be true. One can imagine a society in which everybody is exploited because the surplus is simply thrown away or used in religious sacrifices rather than being appropriated by a class of exploiters. Because Marx did not have this kind of case in mind, the concept of exploitation ought perhaps to be restricted to situations in which the product of labor is put to some further use. If some are exploited, there must be others who are exploiters.

Usually, for any exploited agent we can point to another who is exploiting him. More precisely, we can point to an exploiter who ends up with the surplus produced by the exploited agent. This need not be the case, however. A small, independent farmer or artisan may be exploited, in the precise Marxian sense, but the surplus he produces may be thinly spread out over all his trade partners. Moreover, he may not even know that he is exploited. To assess his "net exploitation status" we would have to carry out horrendously complicated calculations of the labor value of the goods he consumes. Because even a trained economist would hardly be able to do this, we can safely assume that the agent himself will not. Not being aware that he is exploited, he will not be motivated to revolt by the fact that, objectively speaking, he is. Here, the normatively appropriate notion fails to motivate; in the manager–shareholder case, what motivates is an inappropriate notion.

Marx's labor theory of exploitation shares some of the weaknesses of the labor theory of value. By requiring us to compare the amount of labor a person performs and the amount embodied in the goods he consumes, it presupposes that all labor can be reduced to a common denominator. We know, however, that in the presence of inborn skill differences among workers, or differences in irksomeness among jobs, this reduction cannot be carried out. One might argue, along the lines of some pre-Marxian socialists, that the first problem is irrelevant. Inborn skills or talents are morally arbitrary facts that ought not to influence the distribution of earnings. It is just to let wages vary with the number of hours worked, which is within the control of the person, but not with the quality of labor performed, which is not. Although not a theory of exploitation in Marx's sense, this would be a theory of economic justice using labor time as the sole criterion. It cannot, however, handle the second difficulty. If, of two unskilled workers, one has a job which is more dirty and unpleasant than the other, he will be and should be paid more.

For some purposes these problems may be neglected. There is sufficient similarity among workers and among jobs to justify the use of a simplified model. The labor theory of exploitation is something of a straitjacket, because it forces us to render comparable what is not, but then this comment would apply to any scientific model. In any case, it will turn out that even on its own simplifying assumptions the theory is open to serious objections.

## EXPLOITATION, FREEDOM, AND FORCE

How does exploitation arise? Do the exploiters have to force or coerce the exploited? Or could the relation be one of free and voluntary exchange?

Exploitation of slaves and serfs almost invariably rests on physical coercion. Although slaves have sometimes refused freedom when given the option, their preference for slavery in these cases was an effect of the condition of slavery, not its cause. Instances of free men selling themselves into slavery exist, but we may doubt whether their choice was uncoerced. As the French medieval historian Marc Bloch once asked, "In social life is there any more elusive notion than the free will of a small man?"

It has been seriously argued that serfdom rested on a mutually beneficial contract between lord and serfs, with the lord providing military protection in exchange for the serfs' surplus labor. The argument fails, because serfdom was more like a protection racket than a genuine exchange. A gangster who offers protection to a restaurant owner does indeed protect the owner against rival gangsters who would otherwise move in, but no one could seriously argue that the owner is not coerced. The offer-threat is "If you pay us, we will protect you against our rivals; if you don't, we'll punish you." The restaurant owner would be better off were there no gangsters at all, although, given their existence, it is preferable to pay a steady fee to one of them than to be permanently exposed to raids and predation.

The origin of capitalist exploitation cannot be captured in any simple formula. According to Marx, it typically arises because workers are forced by economic circumstances to sell their labor power. They have no land they can cultivate: neither do they have the capital necessary to set themselves up in business. Nor do they usually have the documented entrepreneurial skills that could persuade a bank to lend them money. All alternatives to wage labor – starving, begging, stealing, or the workhouse – are so unattractive that no man in his senses would choose them. The choice of wage labor is forced, although uncoerced.

Coercion presupposes the existence of an exploiter who, deliberately, goes out of his way to increase the likelihood that the agent will choose exploitation over the alternatives. Thus, in slavery and serfdom the exploiters attach severe penalties to the attempt to escape exploitation. In capitalism, this form of physical coercion is rare. Capitalist exploitation can, however, rest on economic coercion, if the capitalist interferes with alternative employment opportunities for the workers. Marx argued that the English enclosures from the sixteenth to the eighteenth century were partly carried out with a view to drive the small peasants from the land, thus coercing them into selling their labor power. Another example of economic coercion would be if capitalist firms deliberately made life difficult for workers' cooperatives, for instance by underselling them more than is normal competitive practice.

The distinction between coercion and what Marx called "the dull force of economic circumstances" is clear enough. Coercion presupposes, and force excludes, intentional efforts by the exploiter to influence the alternatives (other than exploitation) open to the exploited. The distinction between physical and economic coercion is more tenuous, although not unimportant. Physical coercion is illegal in capitalism, whereas economic coercion can employ perfectly legal means. Physical coercion involves the invasion of the rights of others, economic coercion the abuse of one's own rights. Such abuse is often punishable if the motive is sheer spite but usually not if the motive is to make money out of the transaction. If I erect a fence on my property for the sole purpose of shutting off your view, I act spitefully and possibly actionably. If my purpose is to make you pay me not to erect it, it is less clear that what I am doing is legally objectionable. Even when the abuse is illegal, it can be punished only if intent is demonstrated, which may be difficult.

So far we have distinguished three degrees of involuntariness: physical coercion, economic coercion, and being forced by circumstances. Contrary to Marx's belief, exploitation need not be involuntary in any of these senses. Consider two reasons why wives who have stayed at home may decide to enter the labor market. In a recession, the loss of family income may force the wife to sell her labor power. In a boom, the offer of very high wages may induce her to do so. Although she will have less leisure, its value will be enhanced by the money she can spend on it. Living on her husband's income remains an acceptable alternative, but she prefers to work for a wage and, hence, to be exploited. Writing in the mid-nineteenth century, Marx was largely justified in neglecting such cases, but today it is less plausible to assert that all sale of labor power is either coerced or forced.

Neoclassical economists rarely refer to exploitation, and when they do, it is in a sense quite different from the Marxist one. They define exploitation as a wage that is less than the value of the marginal product of labor, whereas Marx would say that there is exploitation when the wage is below the average product of labor. On the neoclassical definition, exploitation is impossible in perfectly competitive capitalism. It arises only when firms have some degree of market power, that is, when they are able to influence wages or prices instead of having to take them as given. The definition is somewhat implausible if we want to retain the usual connotations of exploitation. Assume that a firm happens to have such a large market share that its behavior can affect prices but that the wage rate is given. The firm will not find it profitable to produce up to the point where the value of the marginal product equals the wage, but because its behavior does not affect the wage it is strange to say the workers are thereby exploited.

There is a superficial verbal similarity between Marx's view that exploitation arises because workers are forced to sell their labor power and the neoclassical view that it occurs because firms exercise economic power. On closer inspection, however, the two theories have nothing in common. For one thing, they rest on different concepts of exploitation; for another, workers may be forced to sell their labor power even if there is perfect competition so that no firms have any market power. The fundamental difference is that Marx wanted to argue that exploitation must exist in any form of capitalism, not just in its imperfect forms.

### EXPLOITATION IN HISTORY

The historical varieties of exploitation are numerous and diverse. Exploitation can occur in capitalist as well as precapitalist societies; in market as well as nonmarket economies; in class societies as well as in societies without class divisions.

The simplest variety is exploitation without class formation, which arises in what Marx called "simple commodity production." This is a community of farmers and artisans who own their means of production and employ only family labor. Although there are no labor and credit markets, there is a commodity market where the producers exchange their products with each other. For simplicity we may assume that their goal is to obtain a given level of consumption – the same for all producers – with a minimum of work. It is then intuitively clear, and can be proved rigorously, that if some producers have more capital endowments than others they will have to work fewer hours to get the income needed to achieve the consumption target.

One might question whether this is exploitation. To see that it is, consider another economy that differs from simple commodity production only in that the producers do not trade with each other. Each family produces its own consumption goods. As before, the goal is to achieve a fixed level of consumption with a minimum of work; as before, some are better endowed than others; as before, these will have to work less to achieve their goal. For each of these economies, we carry through the thought experiment of imagining that the poorly endowed producers disappear from the economy, taking their endowments with them. In the no-trade economy the producers who remain behind will work the same number of hours as before. Because they did not interact with the poorly endowed producers, they are not affected by their disappearance. In simple commodity production the better-endowed producers will have to work more under the thought experiment, because they lose the gains from trade. As a group, the better-endowed producers now consume goods that embody exactly as much labor as they perform. When previously they consumed the same goods and worked less, they must have been exploiters. Yet there are no class divisions in this society, because all producers stand in the same relation to the means of production. It is irrelevant that some are rich and some are poor, for wealth is not a Marxist criterion of class.

Marx did not see simple commodity production as a significant historical phenomenon, and for good reasons. In an economy of this kind, the poorly endowed producers will usually lead a highly precarious existence. They are vulnerable to price fluctuations, accidents of weather, illness, and so on. In a crisis they will borrow from the rich producers or offer themselves for hire. In either case a class division is created. Exploitation without class is not a stable situation. Yet it is a logically conceivable situation, which shows that – contrary to a widespread Marxist belief – exploitation and class are not necessarily tied to each other.

Actually, classless exploitation is more than a mere logical possibility. It arises in "unequal exchange" between nations, when rich countries exchange goods with low labor content against goods with high content. Although there may be class divisions within each country, the relation between them is not one of class. Exploitation without class could also occur in market socialism of the Yugoslav variety. Here all workers are members of self-managed firms, so there are no class differences. Yet because of differences in endowments there can arise regional and sectoral inequalities that reveal the presence of exploitation.

In the overwhelming majority of cases, nevertheless, exploitation is accompanied by class divisions. Slaves form a distinct class because they do not own any means of production, not even their own labor power. Serfs have only partial ownership of their labor power, because part of the week they are obliged – on pain of physical coercion – to work on the lord's land. Because the rest of the week they work on plots of their own, they also have partial ownership of their nonlabor means of production. Workers in capitalism have full ownership of their labor power but typically do not own any other means of production.

These are the main relationships of exploitation and class: between slave and slaveowner, serf and lord, worker and capitalist. Yet in societies where one of these was the dominant relation, there have usually existed, alongside it, relations of indebtedness arising in the credit market. Marx claimed that in classical antiquity the conflict between debtor and creditor was the main form of class struggle. More generally, in all precapitalist societies one observes usurer's capital, which has "the mode of exploitation of capital without its mode of production." Even in capitalism proper this form of exploitation persists. Marx argued in *The Eighteenth Brumaire* that the apparently independent French peasantry was in reality exploited by financial capital, through mortgage interests.

Exploitation through usurer's capital or financial capital gives no impetus to the development of the productive forces, because a moneylender has neither the incentive nor the opportunity to improve the methods of production. He has no incentive, because he is not the "residual claimant" who receives what is left over after payment of fixed expenses. Nor does he have an opportunity, for he is not actively involved in the production process. As the residual claimant, the indebted producer does have an incentive, but because of the small scale of production the opportunities for improvement are limited. An industrial capitalist has both the incentive and the opportunity to introduce new techniques. He is both the residual claimant and the actual organizer of production, which, moreover, takes place on a large scale. This accounts for the uniquely dynamical character of capitalism.

As organizer of the production process, the capitalist or his agent enters into a new relation to the workers. In all forms of capitalist exploitation we find the "formal subsumption of labor under capital." In the early stage of capitalism, this was the main relation between the two classes. Industrial capitalism adds a "real subsumption" – the subordination and lack of autonomy of the worker in the work process. This relation is the object of the day-to-day class struggle in capitalism. Because the labor contract cannot specify in full detail what the worker is to do, and because in any case he might not abide with it unless forced to, there is a need for constant supervision and monitoring of his efforts. Although the worker may have agreed to such supervision as part of the contract, he may still resent it deeply as an attack on his autonomy and dignity.

In this struggle, the worker is not without some bargaining chips of his own. Because of his specific, idiosyncratic knowledge of the production techniques of the firm, he may not be easily replaceable. This may lead the capitalist to replace the optimal techniques with others that create less dependence on skilled workers; at any rate he can threaten to do so. Moreover, the very specificity of the worker's knowledge also makes it difficult for him to find another job. The capitalist, in other words, also has some bargaining power. This kind of struggle is not specifically capitalist. It can be expected in any hierarchically organized industrial economy, capitalist or communist. (The terms and outcome of the struggle will, however, depend on further institutional features. The workers have a stronger position if they have security of employment than if they can easily be fired.) The fact that in modern capitalism we observe both exploitation and subordination should not lead us to confuse them with one another, for one can observe the first without the second (in early capitalism) or the second without the first (in managerial communism).

The exploiter need not be an individual. In many societies the state has engaged in exploitation. Marx argued that in the Asiatic mode of production the state, as the ultimate owner of all land, was the main exploiter. In *The Eighteenth Brumaire* and other writings on France he asserted that the bureaucratic state apparatus was a parasite or a vampire that lived off the labor of the common people. He also argued, however, that in the final analysis the Bonapartist state was instrumental in sustaining the rule of capital over labor. The apparently independent state acted as a lightning rod, in attracting to itself some of the opposition that otherwise would have been directed against capital. The merits and demerits of this analysis will concern us later.

More generally, there are several ways in which the state can enter into the foreground or background of exploitation. In bureaucratic agrarian societies the state has been the main exploiter, with the bureaucracy as the ruling class. In ancient Rome taxes were largely siphoned off to the economically dominant classes, whose main base, however, was private property of land and slaves. In capitalism, Marx argued, the state is the guarantor of exploitation, by protecting the class of exploiters against the exploited and against its own individual members. The protection against the exploited may take the form of direct oppression, the indirect form of acting as a lightning rod for opposition, or the even more indirect form of enacting measures in favor of the exploited in order to provide an appearance of legitimacy. The state can also enhance the efficiency of exploitation, by providing public goods that private exploiters do not find it profitable to create. Finally, in all forms of market exploitation the state is present in the background, to ensure freedom of contract and guarantee private property.

At this point we may try to summarize the complex relations that obtain between exploitation relations and power relations. Nonmarket exploitation immediately rests on power. To have full or partial ownership of the labor power of another person *is* to have power over him. Market exploitation does not rest on power in this direct way, but a number of more indirect connections obtain. When a person sells his labor power, the cause, when it is not the "force of circumstances," may be economic coercion. The power of the state is presupposed as a background to any form of market exploitation. Exploitative relationships may also give rise to power relationships, as when a worker sells his labor power to a capitalist and thereby becomes subject to subordination in the work place.

Nonetheless, exploitation is not a power relationship. Consider, as a limiting case, simple commodity production where the producers can earn a good living just by producing for themselves but prefer to earn even more by engaging in trade with each other. Although the exchange may give rise to exploitation, there is no power involved at all. No producers are compelled by the "force of circumstances" to offer their products on the market or coerced to do so by others. Nor is there any subordination in the production process. Although the power of the state is presupposed as a background condition, it is a relation between the state and each of the producers, not among the latter. Although class relations and power relations are closely connected to exploitation, the three phenomena are distinct – logically and sometimes empirically.

In *Capital I* Marx discusses at some length the determinants of the rate of exploitation in capitalism. This rate is defined as the ratio of surplus value to the value of labor power. The latter depends on the real wage and the labor content of the goods that enter into the real wage. Hence, the rate of exploitation depends on the length of the working day, the real wage, and the labor value of goods. Of these, the first two are objects of the class struggle, whereas the third can change only through general technical progress. A cheapening of consumption goods nevertheless has an impact on the class struggle, by modifying the bargaining terms of the parties.

A long chapter is devoted to the struggle over the length of the working day in England, culminating in a discussion of the Ten Hours Bill that was passed in 1848. Marx's analyses of this event are both powerful and incoherent. He offers, in fact, three separate explanations without making it clear how they are related to each other.

First, he argues that the bill passed because it was in the interest of "society," represented by the government. The excessive exploitation of the workers through long working days was threatening the vital forces of the nation. Overworked and underfed workers make bad soldiers. Their poor living conditions were a breeding ground for epidemics, which in turn threatened the other classes as well.

Next, Marx claimed that the bill was carried because of the active efforts of the working class, supported by the landowning aristocracy. Although the latter did not in themselves have an interest in a shorter working day for the workers, they needed their help in their own struggle against the capitalists over the proposed repeal of the Corn Laws. The repeal, by allowing for import of cheap Continental grain, would reduce the price of food and thereby modify the bargaining terms between labor and capital in favor of the latter. The landowners, needless to say, wanted to retain their monopoly power. They could offer the workers their assistance in wearing down capitalist opposition to the Ten Hours Bill, in return for working-class support in regard to the Corn Laws. Marx's analysis of this triangular class relation, with multiple opportunities for alliance formation and strategic behavior, was one of his most important achievements.

Finally, and somewhat perplexingly, Marx suggests that there was no capitalist opposition to the bill. On the contrary, the bill was passed because it was in the interest of the capitalist class as a whole, although contrary to that of each individual capitalist. On this view, the capitalists were placed in a Prisoner's Dilemma. The excessive exploitation of the workers threatened their physical survival and hence the continued existence of the capitalist system itself. It was in the collective interest of the capitalist class not to kill off the goose that was laying the golden eggs. Yet any individual capitalist had always an incentive to exploit his workers to the hilt. If other capitalists showed more moderation, he could gain an edge on them in competition by exploiting his workers more heavily; and he would be only marginally hurt by the ravages he thereby caused. If other capitalists acted according to short-term greed, he would be forced to follow suit, on pain of bankruptcy. Again, this is a powerful analysis, but somewhat flawed, as Marx does not explain how the capitalists overcame their free-rider problem. To say that the Ten Hours Bill was passed because it was in the interest of "capital" would be to commit the twin mistakes of methodological holism and unsupported functional explanation. It is, moreover, difficult to reconcile this account with the others.

Marx had no good explanation of the real wage rate. The problem is in itself very difficult, and in addition Marx suffered from a self-imposed handicap. His view that labor power is a commodity that is produced with specific amounts of consumption goods as inputs led him to the absurdly mechanistic view that, when technical progress leads to a fall in the value of consumption goods, wages must also fall, automatically and proportionally. In reality, when capitalists and workers bargain over the benefits made possible by cheaper consumption goods there is no reason to think that the capitalist will end up with everything. To some extent, Marx recognizes this fact when he refers to a "historical and moral element" in the value of labor power. Yet he does not provide an explanation of why wages differ across countries or over time. He asserts that they are determined by the class struggle and not simply by the play of supply and demand in a perfectly competitive labor market. Yet he does not provide a theory of bargaining that could lend some predictive and explanatory power to this assertion. To some extent, he is absolved by the failure of any later economist to do much better.

The intensity of labor also enters into the determination of the rate of exploitation. To make the workers work harder is in many respects like making them work longer. Both methods increase the amount of labor extracted from the workers in any given twenty-four-hour period. Both have similar effects on the rate at which labor power is worn down and the rate at which it must be compensated. Increasing the intensity of labor does also, however, entail increased costs of supervision. Marx argues, therefore, that piece wages are more suited to capitalist production, because they force the workers to police themselves, at no cost to the capitalist. He forgets that complex industrial technology often requires the cooperation and coordination of many workers, in a way that does not lend itself to piece wages because there are no "pieces" that can be attributed to the individual worker. An alternative would be to have the workers police each other. In part this is achieved by trade unions. Unionized firms have procedures for grievance and conflict resolution that reduce the scope for individual opposition and sabotage and the need for constant supervision of the workers.

Exploitation is a normative, critical concept. This is less obvious in English than in German, which uses different terms, *ausnützen* and *ausbeuten,* for the neutral sense "making use of" and the critical sense "taking unfair advantage of." Marx uses the latter term, which has unambiguous normative connotations. Also, it is impossible to read the burning pages of *Capital I* without sensing Marx's indignation at the practices he is describing. The conclusion is almost unavoidable that part of Marx's indictment of capitalism rests on its injustice. It is unfair that some should be able to earn an income without working, whereas others must toil to eke out a miserable existence.

Yet Marx explicitly denies that he is advocating a particular conception of justice. He asserts that theories of morality and justice are ideological constructions, which only serve to justify and perpetuate the existing property relations. Actions are said to be just or unjust according to a moral code corresponding to a particular mode of production. In capitalism, slavery and fraud are unjust; the extraction of surplus labor is not. There is no transhistorical, nonrelativistic conception of justice. Nor is there a communist theory of justice. Rather, communism will be a society beyond justice. For similar reasons he also rejected the view that communism substitutes altruist motivations for selfish ones and asserted that the very distinction between altruism and egoism will be transcended in communism.

It remains a puzzle how Marx could hold these views and also characterize capitalism and communism in terms that strongly suggest a particular conception of justice. One is left with the answer, although it is difficult to accept when interpreting a writer of Marx's stature, that he did not really understand what he was doing. He was a bit like M. Jourdain, the title character in Molière's play *Le Bourgeois Gentilhomme,* who is astonished to learn that he has been speaking prose all his life without knowing that he was doing anything so fancy. Unlike M. Jourdain, however, Marx went out of his way to refute the correct description of what he was doing.

There are several reasons why Marx felt compelled to deny that one could talk about justice in a meaningful, nonrelativistic way. He was strongly repelled by sanctimonious phrases about justice that served only to legitimate the horrible practices of capitalism. He was also very hostile to moral or moralizing conceptions of communism, believing them to be reactionary in effect if not in intent. More deeply, his attitude is explained by the Hegelian and teleological roots of his thought. He believed that historical development was governed by laws of motion operating with iron necessity, so that moral condemnations were either pointless or superfluous. Communism cannot come about before conditions are objectively ready for it; and when they are, capitalism will fall away by itself. As long as exploitation is historically necessary, it will remain; as soon as its time is past, it will disappear. In neither stage is there a room for moral strictures.

These are highly implausible views. They constitute what is sometimes called scientific socialism, by far the least scientific part of Marx's thought. To see what is wrong with them, we can begin by distinguishing between two senses of "socially necessary exploitation." On the one hand, one might argue that exploitation is socially necessary if an attempt to reduce or eliminate it would defeat its purpose by hurting the very people it was supposed to benefit. With less exploitation the exploited would be worse off: Although less exploited, they would suffer in income or welfare. On the other hand, exploitation could be said to be socially necessary when a reduction would endanger the prospects of the future communist society, even if it would improve the welfare of those currently exploited. The first idea is similar to that proposed by John Rawls in *A Theory of Justice:* Deviations from equality are tolerable as long as they work to the benefit of the worst-off group in society. It might be necessary, for instance, to pay skilled people more than others, in order to induce them to use their socially valuable talents.

The second idea was embraced by Marx, with a twist. He believed exploitation to be necessary in two distinct senses: It was both inevitable and indispensable. Moreover, it was inevitable *because* it was indispensable. He never doubted that the advent of communism was certain. He was confident that exploitation was a necessary condition for communism. Hence, he could conclude that it was indeed inevitable. There are several reasons why he believed exploitation to be an indispensable stepping-stone to communism. The majority must work more than is needed for their subsistence to ensure free time for a creative minority. Without exploitation the artistic and scientific achievements of the past would have been impossible. The development of the productive forces requires the relentless operation of the profit motive, at least up to the point when that very development has created the material conditions for a society in which further development can take place as part of the general self-realization of the individuals. Finally, the existence of a mass of exploited workers creates the indispensable subjective condition for a communist revolution, at the very time when the material conditions are being created. Hence, one can understand why Marx was fond of citing a verse by Goethe:

> Sollte diese Qual uns quälen,
> Da sie unsre Lust vermehrt,
> Hat nicht Myriaden Seelen
> Timur's Herrschaft aufgezehrt?
>
> [Should this torture torment us
> Since it brings us greater pleasure?
> Were not through the rule of Timur
> Souls devoured without measure?]

This detached attitude to the sufferings of mankind contrasts strangely with the indignation Marx expressed in many other places. It is also quite unacceptable. For one thing, it neglects the fact that individuals who live here and now have *rights* that prevent us from sacrificing them as pawns in a wider historical game. For another, even if we disregard the issue of rights and consider the matter as a pure utilitarian calculus, the sacrifice of those currently living for the sake of future generations cannot be justified, except on the unjustifiable assumption that we can know *for cer-*

*tain* that it is sufficient and necessary to bring about communism (as Marx conceived it). Perhaps the most disastrous part of the legacy of Marxism is the intellectual hubris involved in the belief that one can know and predict with confidence the outcome of current conflicts and, indeed, use that knowledge to justify the strategies adopted in the struggle.

It is time to look at the evidence on the other side. What are the reasons for believing that Marx entertained a conception of justice? What is that conception? Is it plausible? There are two kinds of textual evidence to be considered. On the one hand, we must consider what Marx says about capitalism to get a clue to the sense in which it might be unjust. On the other hand, we need to look at his far less numerous statements about communism to see whether they offer a positive conception of justice.

Quite generally, almost any page in *Capital,* opened at random, conveys a very strong impression that Marx is arguing the case for the prosecution in moral terms. More specifically, he frequently refers to the capitalist extraction of surplus value as theft, embezzlement, robbery, and stealing. These are terms that immediately imply that an injustice is being committed. Moreover, the sense in which it is an injustice cannot be the relativistic one. Marx insists that, with respect to capitalist conceptions of justice, exploitation, unlike cheating and fraud, is fair. The sense in which extraction of surplus value is unfair must refer to a nonrelativistic, transhistorical conception. This argument is one important piece of evidence that Marx thought capitalism to be unjust. It is supported by a rare explicit statement from the 1861–3 *Critique,* where Marx says that capitalism will disappear when labor recognizes that the products are its own and that its separation from the means of production is an injustice. Each worker has the right to his own product, or at least its labor time equivalent. Capitalism is an unjust system because some get more and others less than they have contributed.

The main evidence for Marx's conception of justice in communism is, paradoxically, also a main source for the view that Marx had no such conception. This is the *Critique of the Gotha Program,* in which Marx makes an influential distinction between two stages of communism. The full communist society cannot emerge directly from capitalism. In a first stage people will still be dominated by a capitalist mentality, including, among other things, the refusal to work unless paid a proportional wage. Hence, in this stage the principle of distribution is "To each according to his contribution." In the higher stage this constraint disappears. Work itself becomes "the prime want" of life; the springs of social wealth "flow more abundantly"; and society can "inscribe on its banner: From each according to his ability, to each according to his needs."

The contribution principle, according to Marx, is flawed in a way that the needs principle is not. It embodies a bourgeois conception of formal rights that is insensitive to the actual needs of individuals. One who has the capacity to work harder or longer than others also earns more, although that person's needs may be no greater than the needs of others. For equal amounts of work a worker who has a family to support earns the same income as one who does not, although their needs are clearly different. These defects are eliminated in the higher stage of communism. According to Marx, this represents a transition from a society governed by rights to a society in which rights and justice no longer have any role to play.

His argument (somewhat reconstructed) that distribution according to rights is necessarily inadequate goes as follows. A code of justice singles out various properties of persons as criteria for distributing goods among them. Because a code must be written and explicit, it can list only a finite number of properties. Human variety and diversity, on the other hand, are limitless. Two individuals who are alike in all the respects mentioned by the code could nevertheless differ in other respects. Any code of justice must treat unequal individuals equally. If the respects in which the individuals differ are relevant for the distribution of goods among them, the code of justice will produce unjust results. Because the range of potentially relevant features is also limitless, one cannot ensure ahead of application of the code that it will invariably yield the right results.

The argument is self-defeating in an obvious way. Marx is arguing in prose against the possibility of speaking prose. The reference to "defects" in the contribution principle presupposes a normative criterion, that is, a superior principle of justice. To reject one principle Marx must appeal to another. The contribution principle is assessed in light of the needs principle. Although Marx does not say in so many words what the latter amounts to, the most natural interpretation, given the examples he adduces to refute the contribution principle, is that goods ought to be distributed so as to equalize welfare. This is a well-known theory of justice, which certainly cannot serve the function of refuting the possibility of a theory of justice.

The valid core in Marx's argument is that, when it comes to implementing a theory of justice, one has to rely on a finite number of observable properties. This is equally true for distribution according to needs. The welfare of individuals cannot be observed directly, as if they were walking around with a "hedonometer" attached to them. Distribution must be regulated by observable features of individuals that are known to have a general correlation with the ability to achieve welfare. In any given case, the correlation might not hold, or it might hold only imperfectly. A person with a physical handicap (for which he is not compensated) might live a much happier life than most people. Conversely, people with extraordinary artistic or scientific gifts might live lives of misery because they, much better than others, are able to see how far their achievements fall short of their ideals. Such examples show only that when applying a theory of justice it is absurd to search for fine-tuned perfection. Any attempt to approach perfect equality of welfare would probably defeat its purpose, because of the costs involved in an exact assessment of who needs what.

We are still left with another puzzle. Marx's analysis of capitalism condemns exploitation by appealing to the principle "To each according to his labor contribution." Marx's analysis of communism condemns that very principle by appealing to the principle "To each according to his needs." The puzzle can be resolved by imputing to Marx a two-tier or hierarchical theory of justice. The ideal or first-best conception is distribution according to needs. In the lower state of communism, as it emerges out of capitalism, people will still act on selfish motives. Moreover, work will still be drudgery and offer few opportunities for self-realization. Implementing the needs principle under these conditions would be disastrous, because no one would be motivated to work hard. There would be, in fact, a Prisoner's Dilemma: All would benefit by all working hard, but without a link between individual contribution and individual reward all would prefer to shirk. To overcome this problem one must create a link between effort and reward; this is what the contribution principle does. It is a pragmatic or second-best approximation to the ideal of equal welfare. It promotes equality because it prescribes equal pay for equal work, although it also violates equality by allowing equal pay for unequal needs. If an able-bodied capitalist earns an income without working, it is a violation of the contribution principle that cannot be justified by the needs principle. Exploitation is condemned by the first-best as well as by the second-best principle of distributive justice.

The theory I have constructed, on the basis of some of Marx's writings, can be challenged on many grounds. One may appeal to other of his writings to argue that he did not hold any theory of justice. I have given my reasons for thinking that this argument cannot be decisive. More relevantly, one might argue against the theory itself. One might object, first, that the contribution principle does not allow us to understand what is wrong about exploitation; second, that it is not the best pragmatic approximation to the needs principle; and third, that the needs principle itself is indefensible.

The contribution principle tells us that exploitation is always and inherently unjust. Here are two counterexamples. Consider first an interaction between two individuals who differ in two respects. Although both have some capital, one has more than the other. The one who has less capital likes to have a lot of leisure but does not care much about income; the other has the opposite priority. It could then happen that the first does not even work up all his capital, whereas the second has used up hers. The second would then offer to sell her labor power to the first. The poor person, in other words, exploits the rich person. It would be contrary to all our intuitions to say that the poor person is acting objectionably. This kind of situation probably does not arise frequently, but there is nothing wildly improbable about it. It demonstrates, I think conclusively, that exploitation is not inherently wrong.

The second counterexample is more controversial but also more relevant for real-life problems. Consider two persons who have the same skills and capital endowments but differ in the importance they attach to present as opposed to future consumption. One of them is more willing to postpone consumption than the other. She will save part of her earning and accumulate more capital, whereas the other spends all his current income. After some time the first has accumulated more capital than she can profitably use. She will offer the other to work for her, at a wage that exceeds what he could gain by himself. True, he will be exploited – but who cares? In Robert Nozick's phrase, what is wrong about "capitalistic acts between consenting adults"? Both benefit from the transaction, and nobody else is harmed. The example suggests that exploitation is legitimate when the unequal capital endowments have a "clean" causal history. Actual cases will be less clear-cut, but I do not think one can block the argument by asserting that it will never apply in reality.

These counterexamples do not show that exploitation, in the typical case, is not morally objectionable. Nor do they detract from the usefulness of the notion in broader historical analyses. Exploitation in history has almost always had a thoroughly unclean causal origin, in violence, coercion, or unequal opportunities. What they show is that exploitation is not a fundamental moral concept. Exploitation, when objectionable, is so because of specific features of the situation that are not always present. Further work ought to focus on these features while continuing to study exploitation as an important special case.

The contribution principle, therefore, is not a good tool for fine-tuned investigations into the morality of capitalism. Nor is it a very good approximation to the ideal of equality of welfare. A better pragmatic compromise – one that takes account of the selfish motivations of most individuals – is John Rawls's proposal that institutions ought to be arranged so as to make the worst-off as well off as possible. Or one might advocate the slightly different proposal that inequalities of welfare are to be tolerated as long as they make everybody better off. Both of these are more in the spirit of welfare egalitarianism than the contribution principle. Because that principle does not allow for redistributive taxation, it could lead to quite large welfare inequalities. The comparison is admittedly somewhat artificial, because Marx's description of the first stage of communism has too little structure to allow us to deduce what the distributions of income and welfare could look like. Yet, with respect to any given structure, it would be true that Rawls's principle, or something like it, would yield the best approximation to equality of welfare.

Take, finally, the principle "To each according to his needs." It is sometimes argued that by satisfaction according to needs Marx meant that each and every person would be able to satisfy each and every need to the point of satiation. Through a combination of material abundance and the elimination of needs that are inherently insatiable, individuals would be able to take what they wanted, when they wanted it, from the common stock of goods. There is some textual evidence for imputing this extremely utopian conception to Marx, but I believe that it is not only more charitable but also more plausible to interpret the needs principle as a statement of welfare egalitarianism.

As a first-best theory of justice, that view is very attractive. Welfare is what we care about directly; income and other resources matter only to the extent that they provide us with welfare. Also, there is a general presumption in favor of equality that places the burden of proof on its opponents. There are many problems – of information, motivation, and decision costs – that stand in the way of untrammeled equality of welfare, but these, one might argue, are irrelevant for the construction of an ideal theory.

In reply one might want to question the relevance of a theory that is so ideal that it has to abstract from some of the most fundamental features of the human condition, but this is not the objection I want to pursue here. Rather, I want to point to one consequence of welfare egalitarianism that seems to run strongly counter to our ethical intuitions. If some people have desires, tastes, preferences, or plans that are very expensive to realize, they would have to get a disproportionate amount of society's scarce resources. It is hard to accept that this would be a fair allocation. An expensive taste is not like a handicap, for which people ought justly to be compensated. Society must reserve itself the right to warn its members that if they develop expensive tastes they will not be able to satisfy them to the extent needed to guarantee equality of welfare. As a result, people will on the whole cultivate less expensive tastes than if their satisfaction had been underwritten by society (to the extent compatible with equal welfare for all). A further consequence is that people will on the whole achieve higher welfare levels, because the scarce resources can now be used to greater effect.

### BIBLIOGRAPHY

*Introduction.* The best treatments of exploitation are found in a book and several articles by John Roemer: *A General Theory of Exploitation and Class* (Harvard University Press, 1982); "Property relations vs surplus-value in Marxian exploitation," *Philosophy and Public Affairs* 11, (1982): 281–313; "Should Marxists be interested in exploitation?", *Philosophy and Public Affairs* 14 (1985): 30–65.

*Exploitation, freedom, and force.* A useful typology of forms of economic coercion is Y. Lieberman and M. Syrquin, "On the use and abuse of rights," *Journal of Economic Behavior and Organization* 46 (1983): 25–40. The involuntary character of feudal exploitation is argued in S. Fenoaltea, "The rise and fall of a theoretical model: the manorial system," *Journal of Economic History* 35 (1975): 386–409. The question of whether workers are forced (or coerced) to sell their labor power is discussed in G. A. Cohen, "The structure of proletarian unfreedom," *Philosophy and Public Affairs* 12 (1983): 3–33, and D. Zimmerman, "Coercive wage offers," *Philosophy and Public Affairs* 10 (1981): 121–45. An exposition of the neoclassical theory of exploitation is found in M. Bronfenbrenner, *Income Distribution Theory* (Macmillan, 1971).

*Exploitation in history.* An analysis of exploitation among nations is J. Roemer, "Unequal exchange, labour migration, and international capital flows: a theoretical synthesis," in P. Desai (ed.), *Marxism, the Soviet Economy, and Central Planning: Essays in Honor of Alexander Ehrlich* (MIT Press, 1983), pp. 34–60. Some data on income inequality under market socialism are found in S. Estrin, *Self-Management: Economic Theory and Yugoslav Practice* (Cambridge University Press, 1983). An outstanding study of exploitation in classical antiquity is G. E. M. de Ste. Croix, *The Class Struggle in the Ancient Greek World* (Duckworth, 1981). Detailed analyses of the modalities of feudal exploitation are found in several articles by Marc Bloch, reprinted in his *Mélanges Historiques* (Paris: SEVPEN, 1961). An imaginative and stimulating discussion of economic, social, and political aspects of exploitation in nineteenth-century England is Karl Polanyi, *The Great Transformation* (Beacon Press, 1957). The role of trade unions in modern capitalism is well explained in R. B. Freeman and J. L. Medoff, *What Do Unions Do?* (Basic Books, 1984). Their book can be usefully supplemented by O. Williamson, M. Wachter, and J. Harris, "Understanding the employment relation: the analysis of idiosyncratic exchange," *Bell Journal of Economics* 6 (1975): 250–80.

*Exploitation and justice.* The two books that figure prominently in the foreground or background of discussions of this problem are J. Rawls, *A Theory of Justice* (Harvard University Press, 1971), and R. Nozick, *Anarchy, State, and Utopia* (Blackwell, 1974). Recent book-length treatments of the place of moral theory in Marxism include A. Buchanan, *Marx and Justice* (Methuen, 1982), and S. Lukes, *Marxism and Morality* (Oxford University Press, 1985). Good discussions of some specific substantive problems include Roemer, "Should Marxists be interested in exploitation?"; and G. A. Cohen, "Robert Nozick and Wilt Chamberlain," in J. Arthur and W. Shaw (eds.), *Justice and Economic Distribution* (Prentice-Hall, 1978), pp. 246–62. An extensive criticism of welfare egalitarianism is R. Dworkin, "What is equality? Part 1: Equality of welfare," *Philosophy and Public Affairs* 10 (1981): 185–246.

# 6

# HISTORICAL MATERIALISM

## INTRODUCTION

MARX had both an empirical theory of history and a speculative philosophy of history. The former, which has come to be known as historical materialism, is a set of macrosociological generalizations about the causes of stability and change in societies. The latter, largely of Hegelian inspiration, offers a scheme for interpreting all historical events in terms of their contribution to realizing the end of history – in both senses of that term. Communism is both the goal of history and the point at which it comes to rest. Although there may be development and change in communism, it will not involve qualitative transformations of the social structure.

The speculative conception involves a division of history into three stages: preclass society, class society, and postclass society. In a different terminology, the stages are referred to as primitive unity, alienation, and unity-with-differentiation. Historical materialism is an investigation of the middle stage, the historical class societies. Not unsurprisingly, the speculative, teleological thinking impinges on the empirical part of the theory, and especially on the view that the successive sets of property relations in history are nothing but instruments for promoting technical change and thus, ultimately, for preparing communism. A major gap, or flaw, in Marx's theory of history is that he does not provide a plausible mechanism to connect the thirst for surplus labor with the development of the productive forces. Another, related flaw is that he does not spell out why men should have an incentive to change the property relations when and because the existing ones cease to be optimal for the development of the productive forces. In one word, Marx's teleological bent made him think he could dispense with microfoundations.

Historical materialism has two sides to it. On the one hand, it is a general theory of the structure and dynamics of any mode of production; on the other hand, it is a theory of the historical sequence of modes of production. The first is about what all modes of production have in common with each other; the second, about how they differ.

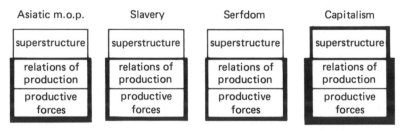

The first of the historical modes of production is the Asiatic one, based on state ownership of land. Then follow the better-known forms of slavery, serfdom, and capitalism. Each of these modes of production has an economic basis and a political and ideological superstructure. In the economic basis we find the relations of production (essentially: property forms) and the productive forces (essentially: technology). By the thickness of the lines in the accompanying table, I have tried to indicate how much Marx wrote about these various aspects of historical development. The economic study of capitalism is, in sheer quantitative terms, by far the most important part of his work. He also wrote a great deal about the politics and ideology of capitalism and about precapitalist economic formations. There is very little about superstructural phenomena in precapitalist societies.

Marx's theory is very unevenly balanced. The general theory is set out in one long, terse paragraph in the preface to *A Critique of Political Economy* and in various rambling, disconnected passages in *The German Ideology*. Because it is formulated at a very high level of abstraction, the central concepts can be elucidated only if we go to Marx's writings on economic history, class struggle, and politics. There, however, we encounter two disconcerting facts. On some points Marx has almost nothing to say. In particular, the paucity of writings on precapitalist politics makes it very difficult to reconstruct a general Marxist theory of the relation between economics and politics. On other points, where Marx does have something to say, what he says appears to be in flat contradiction with the general theory. Some of these inconsistencies are not very serious, but others arise at the very core of the theory. For one thing, the general theory of what drives the transition from one mode of production to another is not borne out by Marx's historical and political writings. For another, the concept of a mode of production is less central in his historical works than one would expect. Instead of the periodization of history into four modes of production based on different forms of exploitation, Marx punctuates history into various stages of the rise and fall of the market.

The most disturbing feature of Marx's historical theories and writings is their lack of integration with one another. We are told three different stories about historical development. There is the story summarized in the opening lines of *The Communist Manifesto:* All history is the history of class struggle. Then there is the equally well-known story set out in the preface to *A Critique of Political Economy:* What history is all about is the development of the productive forces. Finally, there is the account that dominates in the *Grundrisse* and *Capital:* History is the process whereby isolated producers begin to trade with each other, to produce for exchange and ultimately for surplus. Even taken separately, these accounts are shot through with ambiguities and, sometimes, inconsistencies. Taken together, they form a bewildering and confusing picture. It could be, of course, that Marx was fully in control of what he was doing; that he gave us three glimpses of one and the same development, seen from different vantage points. In the absence of a coherent reconstruction, it seems more plausible that he suffered from a severe lack of intellectual control.

## THE DEVELOPMENT OF THE PRODUCTIVE FORCES

Historical materialism is not simply a theory that accords a privileged place to economic factors. It is, more specifically, a form of technological determinism. The rise and fall of successive property regimes are explained by their tendency to promote or fetter technical change. In Marx's language, this is expressed as follows. Within each mode of production, there initially obtains a correspondence between the relations of production and the productive forces. Later the correspondence turns into a contradiction, which causes "an epoch of social revolution" and the setting up of new relations of production, which, for a while, reestablish the correspondence.

For most purposes, the *productive forces* can be taken to mean everything that promotes the mastery of man over nature, for the purpose of want satisfaction. (Thus military technology is not included among the productive forces. There are forms of technological determinism that give prime importance to the means of destruction, but Marx's is not one of them.) Technology, science, and human skills are the most important productive forces. Marx sometimes, but inconsistently with his general theory, also counts sheer manpower as a productive force. The *development* of the productive forces is measured by the degree to which, under constant external conditions, the same goods can be produced with less human labor. Because external conditions may change, such development need not bring about an actual reduction in necessary labor time and human drudgery. Increasing technical sophistication may be offset, for example, by depletion of exhaustible resources. In a full statement of Marx's theory we must take account both of the actual level of productivity and of the hypothetical level that would be reached under constant external conditions.

The *relations of production* are roughly what in non-Marxist language is called property rights, with a few nuances. They include only property of productive forces. The presence of domestic slaves, for instance, is not sufficient to create the relations of production characteristic of slavery, because such slaves are consumption goods rather than productive assets. Also, relations of production need not take the form of legal ownership, backed by state power. In societies with a weak central power the relations of production may just amount to effective control, underwritten by private violence or by a dominant ideology, that stops others from taking over, or even from wanting to take over.

To describe the relations of production in a given society, we must know the answer to the following questions. Do the immediate producers own their labor power, in part or in whole? Do they own their nonlabor means of production, in part or in whole? If they do not, is the owner an individual or a collectivity? Answers to the first two questions allow us to distinguish among slavery, serfdom, simple commodity production, and capitalism. The answer to the last question allows us, in addition, to distinguish between serfdom and the Asiatic mode of production, or between private-property capitalism and state capitalism. The relations of production are also what distinguish the modes of production from one another.

A set of relations of production *corresponds* to the productive forces when it is optimally suited to develop the latter. Now there is no set of relations of production that is optimal for the development of the productive forces under all conditions. What relations are in fact optimal depends on specific historical circumstances. On a first approximation we may say that *the level of development of the productive forces determines what relations are optimal for their further development.* This is not quite accurate, however. To see why, consider the reason why communism, according to Marx, will eventually become a superior framework for developing the productive forces. The material conditions created by capitalism will, under communist conditions, allow the full and free self-realization of the individual and, as a by product, an unprecedented expansion of the productive forces. These material conditions include a large surplus that will make work a matter of free choice rather than necessary drudgery. They cannot, therefore, be stated in terms of the development of the productive forces, because a high level of their development is compatible with a low level of actual productivity.

A *contradiction* between forces and relations of production means, simply, the absence of correspondence. There is contradiction when the existing relations of production are less efficient at developing the productive forces than some other relations would be. This need not imply stagnation. The contradiction sets in when the rate of technical change is smaller than it could have been, not when it becomes smaller than it was previously.[2] What causes the contradiction is the development of the productive forces that took place during the period when the relation was one of correspondence. Any mode of production stimulates a development of the productive forces that will lead to its own obsolescence. Being obsolescent, it will then be thrown on the scrap heap of history and a new one, better suited to the historical task of developing the productive forces, will take its place. A change in the relations of production occurs when and because the existing relations cease to be optimal for the development of the productive forces.

The only substantive assertion in this argument is the claim that a change in the relations of production occurs when and because the existing relations cease to be optimal for the development of the productive forces. As it stands, this is an unsupported functional explanation. Marx owes us an account of how the less than optimal character of the existing relations of production motivates individual men to collective action for the purpose of ushering in a new set of relations. There are good reasons for thinking that it will be hard to come up with such an account. From the point of view of the individual economic agent, the benefits of a change in the property regime are remote in time, subject to uncertainty and independent of his participation in the collective action. Even when there is a "need" for new relations of production, one cannot assume without further argument that it will be fulfilled. Men are not the puppets of history; they act for goals and motives of their own.

When we turn to Marx's writings on the historical modes of production, they do not provide applications and clarifications of the general theory. There is no suggestion that each of the three

---

2 Thus one would be doubly mistaken in thinking that a contradiction can be immediately detected by a decline in the actual surplus. First, the development of the productive forces can be assessed only by a thought experiment, in which the performance of the new technology under the given external conditions is compared with its performance under the previous conditions (when it did not actually exist). Second, the optimal or suboptimal rate of that development can be assessed only by another thought experiment, in which it is compared with the development that would have taken place under different relations of production. All of this amounts to saying that the notion of a contradiction between forces and relations of production is very much a theoretical concept.

precapitalist modes of production divides into a progressive stage, in which the relations of production correspond to the productive forces, and a regressive stage, in which the correspondence becomes a contradiction. On the contrary, Marx says over and over again that technology was essentially unchanging from antiquity to the early modern period, with the exception of the invention of gunpowder, the printing press, and the compass. The destabilizing element in the ancient world was not the development of the productive forces but the growth of population. At times Marx appears to have thought of population as a productive force, so that its growth could be taken as an instance of the development of the productive forces, but this is clearly inconsistent with the general theory. Population growth does not lead to an increase in production per capita, although it may lead to an increase in total production (and in total surplus).

Marx's account of the transition from feudalism to capitalism is very complex, but it also appears to be inconsistent with the general theory. A tentative summary of his thought, or at least one major strand in it, could be the following. Sometime in the sixteenth or seventeenth century the European economies had become unrecognizably changed, compared to the medieval period. Population growth, the discovery of the New World, the invention of modern techniques of warfare, along with the destruction of the military power of the feudal nobility, were the main causes of this transformation. In this new constellation, merchants and producers found that they could increase their surplus by organizing production on a capitalist basis. The necessary conditions were, on the one hand, the creation of a free, landless proletariat and, on the other hand, the accumulation of capital from overseas activities. The surplus extraction took place, essentially, by lowering the real wage, increasing the intensity of work, and extending the length of the working day. For these purposes, it was most efficient to assemble the workers in one place, the factory. Once created, this institution also lent itself to technical change, first somewhat hesitantly and then at an ever-increasing rate.

In this story, the development of the productive forces plays only a tertiary role. The prior transformations of the economy that made capitalist relations optimal did not include technical change, except for improvements in the means of destruction. Moreover, capitalist relations were not introduced because they were optimal for the development of the productive forces but because they allowed for a higher surplus at a given technical level. This is a more plausible account than the general theory, because it immediately provides a link to the motivation of individual economic agents, but it is not, to repeat, consistent with it. The development of the productive forces occurs only as a by-product of the introduction of capitalist relations and not in the explanation of why they came to be introduced.[3]

Consider, finally, Marx's account of the impending transition from capitalism to communism. In this case the general theory becomes especially implausible. Because Marx insisted that technical change in capitalism was accelerating rather than slowing down, he could not argue that capitalism was moribund because stagnating. Rather, he would have to argue that the workers will be motivated by the prospect of a communist society that will allow for technical change at an even higher rate. According to current theories of revolution (and to common sense), this is a highly unlikely motivation. People revolt when things are getting worse or when their expectations of improvement are not fulfilled, or both; but when things go well they do not take to arms simply because of the abstract possibility of a society in which things could go even better.

There are two suggestions in Marx about how to overcome this problem. One is by dropping the second half of the requirement that communism will come about "when and because" communism becomes better suited for the further development of the productive forces. Marx might argue, that is, that the communist revolution will be caused by something other than the contradiction between the forces and relations of production but will still coincide in time with the emergence of that contradiction. The-

---

3 One modification must be added. One way in which capitalist organization of production increased the surplus was by exploiting economies of scale, both in agriculture (through the enclosures of land) and in industry. Although one would not normally refer to this as a form of technical change, it does at least create a link between the introduction of capitalist relations and increases in productivity.

oretical argument and historical experience suggest that this happy coincidence is unlikely. In Trotsky's phrase, "societies are not so rational in building that the dates for proletarian dictatorship arrive exactly at that moment when the economic and cultural conditions are ripe for socialism." Indeed, the opposite seems to be true. To be a breeding ground for revolution, a society must be so backward that any revolution, were it to occur, would be premature from the point of view of the development of the productive forces.

The second suggestion is that communism comes about when capitalism becomes inefficient with respect not to the development but to the use of the productive forces. The productive forces are badly utilized when workers are unemployed, machinery lies idle, and goods produced meet no effective demand. Although the general theory does not warrant the description of such phenomena as a contradiction between the productive forces and the relations of production, Marx referred to them by such phrases and invoked them in his theory of the imminent downfall of capitalism. The objection to this procedure is that there is no guarantee that a society in which the productive forces are more efficiently used will also allow for a higher rate of their development. Indeed, Joseph Schumpeter argued that the dynamic efficiency of capitalism is inseparable from its static inefficiency, so that any attempt to reduce the waste and irrationality of capitalism would also slow it down.

The most fundamental question is, of course, what reasons we have for thinking that a communist society would be superior to capitalism when it comes to technical change. The process of innovation may be dissected into two stages. First, there is a search for new techniques and methods; next, there is the selection of one of the techniques thrown up by the search (or the retention of the old technique if no preferred technique is found). Marx argued that capitalism was consistently inferior to communism with respect to the second stage, because the profit motive could lead capitalists to reject socially desirable innovations. He argued that up to a certain point capitalism was superior to communism with respect to the first stage. The profit motive is one way of generating technical change. Free, spontaneous self-realization is another. The latter, when feasible, is superior, but it becomes feasible only at a high level of development of the productive forces, when men are freed from drudgery. Before that level is reached, capitalism is superior with respect to the intensity of search and, because this is the dominant stage in the process, superior with respect to the net outcome of the two stages.

Schumpeter accepted Marx's argument with respect to the selection efficiency of communism but rejected it with respect to the search efficiency. Today, it seems more reasonable to reject both parts of Marx's contention. The experience of the communist countries suggests that they are clumsy and inefficient both in making use of the productive knowledge they have and in developing new knowledge. To think otherwise, one would have to argue that communism was introduced prematurely in these countries and that the historical experience does not constitute an objection to a theory whose central premise is that it should not be introduced before superiority to capitalism is achieved or within reach. This observation, though in a sense undeniable, is idling as long as one does not provide solid reasons for thinking that there exists a level of the productive forces at which capitalism ceases to become optimal for their further development.

## BASE AND SUPERSTRUCTURE

What is "base" is both lowly and fundamental. Economic activities, on the one hand, have often been seen as a dirty business that no self-respecting man wants to get mixed up with if he can avoid it. On the other hand, though evil, they form a necessary prerequisite for other, nobler activities. The history of materialism is full of such homely truths as Ludwig Feuerbach's "Der Mensch ist was er isst" ("Man is what he eats") or Berthold Brecht's "Erst kommt das Fressen, dann kommt die Moral" ("Food before morals"). Even Marx is capable of such trite statements as "The Middle Ages could not live on Catholicism, nor the ancient world on politics." The first step toward an understanding of the relation between the economic base and the political and intellectual superstructure is to see that it cannot be reduced to, or defended by, these trivially true claims.

The base—superstructure theory is not an assertion that for there to be politics and ideologies at all there also has to be production. It asserts that the *specific* kinds of political and intellectual activities observed in class societies can be explained by reference to equally specific forms of economic organization. Far from being trivially true, it is falsifiable and indeed false. Political and intellectual phenomena have a considerable degree of autonomy. They can also – and note that this is a separate, stronger claim – contribute to explaining economic phenomena. An illustration – whose correctness does not concern us here – is Max Weber's suggestion that an independently arising Protestantism had a causal influence on the development of capitalism. The weak claim would be substantiated by the independence of Protestantism, that is, the lack of an economic explanation; the stronger claim, if it was also shown that it enters into the explanation of economic phenomena.

G. A. Cohen has proposed a powerful, unified interpretation of the two central relations of historical materialism, that between the forces and relations of production and that between base and superstructure. On his account, both are rendered in terms of functional explanation. The relations of production are explained through their beneficial consequences for the development of the productive forces. The legal, political, and intellectual superstructure is similarly explained through its beneficial consequence for the maintenance of the relations of production. In non-Marxist language, politics and ideas are explained by the fact that they stabilize property rights; and property rights are explained by the fact that they give an impetus to technical change.

This does not imply that the superstructure is explained by the fact that, indirectly, it gives an impetus to technical change. The superstructure exercises its stabilizing influence on the relations of production even when they have ceased to be optimal for the further development of the productive forces. This fact, however, creates difficulties for the theory. When the relations of production are no longer explicable in terms of their impact on the productive forces, must the explanation of their persistence be sought in the superstructure? This would appear to contradict the view that the superstructure is explained by its impact on the relations of production. Or should we say that nonfunctional relations of production are explained by the fact that they were once functional, just as nonfunctional properties of organisms are explained by the fact that they were functional in an earlier, different environment? That answer runs into a disanalogy between biology and history: There are no forces that actively resist adaptation in biology, as the superstructure does in society. Or should we say that the existence of a superstructure that explains the persistence of nonfunctional relations of production is itself explained by the fact that it arose at an earlier time to stabilize the relations of production, which, at that time, were independently explained by their impact on the productive forces? That the superstructure, after a certain point, keeps alive what kept it alive? This, again, would accord a more independent role to the superstructure than can be easily accommodated within the theory. The Marxist response tends to be that the superstructure turns out to be weaker "in the long run"; it cannot keep artificially alive forever what has lost the right to live. In the absence of a theory to circumscribe the limits of the long run, this statement is unfalsifiable and, hence, unscientific.

On Cohen's interpretation of Marx, the fact that the superstructure has a causal impact on the base does not exclude that the former could be explained by the latter. If it could be shown, in Weber's example, that Protestantism arose or persisted because of its favorable impact on capitalist relations of production, it would be explained by economic facts beyond itself. Hence the disagreement between Marx and Weber need not be: Did Protestantism exercise a causal influence on capitalism, or was it the other way around? It could also be: Given that Protestantism had a causal impact on capitalism, did it owe its emergence or persistence to that impact?

To assess this view, one must first decide what to mean by "superstructure." First, one can mean all the phenomena that can be functionally explained by their stabilizing impact on the relations of production. Prior to empirical investigation, the superstructure might, for all we know, be empty. Or it might turn out to include everything noneconomic, as in the somewhat paranoid explanations of certain Marxists who have explained the most unlikely phenomena – from criminal behavior to the doctrines of other Marxists immediately to their left or right – by their stabilizing impact on capitalist domination.

Second, the superstructure could be defined as the set of phenomena that can be explained – functionally or otherwise – in terms of the economic structure of society. In addition to the phenomena covered by the first definition, this would include such facts as the following. Sometimes the distribution of political power derives in an immediate, transparent way from the distribution of economic resources: The economically dominant class concentrates political power in its own hands. Perhaps surprisingly, this arrangement can work against the interest of the class. If they fall victim to short-term greed, they can undermine their economic power by abuse of their political power. This was the pattern, for instance, of politics in ancient Rome, where the powerful senators-landowners used state revenues as an additional source of income, at the expense of public goods and defense. Although this arrangement was not optimal for the relations of production, it is still explained by them. For another example, consider the tendency of beliefs to become distorted by class interest or class position. When the victims of this tendency are members of the economically dominant class, their distorted beliefs, although explained by the relations of production, do not reinforce them. In the phrase of the French historian Paul Veyne, beliefs born of passion serve passion badly.

Third, one might simply define the superstructure as all non-economic phenomena. This procedure is unsatisfactory, because it easily lends itself to verbal juggling. One may, for instance, first define a phenomenon as superstructural on the grounds that it is noneconomic and then simply assume that it can be explained by economic phenomena because the superstructure must be supported by something more fundamental, the economic base. If this definition is adopted, one must at least take care not to prejudge the question of whether the superstructural phenomena are dependent on the economic base.

Of these, I think the second definition accords best with the Marxist tradition. If we can demonstrate that a set of widely held beliefs arises directly out of certain economic interests, even if those beliefs do not serve the latter, most Marxists would probably relegate them to the superstructure. The definition sometimes goes together with the view that the superstructure, thus defined, exhausts all noneconomic phenomena. The contrast with the first definition, adopted by Cohen, is not just a question of words. The important substantive issue involved is whether there are phenomena that fall under the second definition but not under the first. If there are not, functional explanation would indeed be as central to Marxism as claimed by Cohen. If there are, as seems undeniable, it cannot be taken as the privileged form of explanation in historical materialism.

A conceptual problem arises in the Asiatic mode of production and, more generally, in any society in which the state bureaucracy is the main exploiting class. Here the relations of production appear to coincide immediately with the political relations – "rent and tax coincide" – so that it is difficult to see how the latter could be explained by the former. A cause and its effect must be distinct entities. Because Marx wrote so little about superstructural phenomena in precapitalist societies, it is impossible to reconstruct an answer to this puzzle from his writings. Most probably, there is no answer. The theory of base and superstructure is a generalization from societies where it is at least meaningful (which is not to say that it is true) to other societies in which it cannot even be coherently stated.

Marx lived and wrote in a society in which economic and political activities were extremely dissociated. In mid-nineteenth-century England they were carried out by two distinct sets of people: Workers did not vote, and capitalists took little interest in politics. Similarly, in ancient Athens slaves were, of course, excluded from politics, as were the foreigners who carried on trade and commerce. In such societies the base–superstructure distinction is immediately meaningful. It also makes some sense, albeit more tenuously, in societies where the same people are involved in both economics and politics, in different social roles. In modern capitalist societies, one can be a worker and also a voter, a businessman and also a member of parliament. The distinction breaks down, however, in societies where economic and political power coincide immediately. Contemporary Soviet Russia is a dramatic example. In this society there is no independent set of economic relations that determines the political superstructure; politics is everywhere.

## THE STAGES OF HISTORICAL DEVELOPMENT

To impose some order on the chaotic appearance of historical change, it is tempting to assimilate it to other, known phenomena. The organic metaphors of birth, growth, maturity, decay, and death present themselves immediately. So do various geometrical analogies, which allow us to see history as linear, circular, or spiral. The *line* underlies images of history as based on constant, uninterrupted progress. The *circle* corresponds to visions of the eternal return, the rise and fall of empires in an unchanging cycle. The *spiral* is a more complex notion. It involves the idea of a cycle superimposed upon a linear trend, of history repeating itself at ever-higher levels. The linear model can be summarized as "one step forward, and then one more step forward"; the circular view as "one step forward, one step backward." Depending on one's perspective, the spiral can be seen either as "one step backward, two steps forward" or as "two steps forward, one step backward."

As practiced especially by nineteenth-century writers, these analogies had a disastrous influence. They distracted attention from the task of grounding historical processes in the actions and motivations of individual men and focused instead on ways of fitting the changes into some wider pattern. They made it legitimate to explain history from above rather than from below. This is not to say that there are no such patterns in history, only that, if there are, an argument is needed to show that they are not a mere coincidence. One must show, that is, that they can be expected to arise, under a wide range of circumstances, as the unintended consequence of the behavior of individuals acting for goals of their own. Patterns must be explained: They do not provide an explanation of anything.

Marx's three-stage philosophy of history illustrates the pattern "One step backward, two steps forward." The primitive communities must be destroyed before community can be re-created at a higher level. Historical materialism asserts that the successive stages in this destruction are also the carriers of an uninterrupted development of the productive forces. As the producers become increasingly separated from their means of production, their labor becomes more productive. Separation is carried to the extreme in capitalism, which is also the stage in which the development of the productive forces reaches its highest level.

What is, within this general scheme, the significance of the successive modes of production? Granted the necessity of capitalism, was each of the three precapitalist modes of production an equally necessary step in the development of humanity toward communism? Marx seems committed to an affirmative answer but does not really offer any arguments for it. He does not, for instance, explain why the Asiatic mode of production could not by itself have changed into a more decentralized system of serfdom, without the intermediate stage of slavery; or – to anticipate what he might have responded – why serfdom could not have given rise to capitalism without a prior stage of slavery.

The puzzle becomes even more complicated when we turn to a quite different periodization of history, which Marx employs alongside the sequence of modes of production. In the *Grundrisse* and in *Capital* Marx argues that the module of historical development is *the rise and fall of the market*. This process occurs twice in the history of mankind.[4] The first time it coincides with the Asiatic and the ancient modes of production; the second time, with feudalism and capitalism. Although Marx's descriptions of the sequence fluctuate somewhat, it appears to be punctuated by five main stages.

The first stage is production for immediate consumption within a small community of producers. There is no trade or reinvestment of a surplus. The transition to the second stage occurs when members of different communities accidentally come into contact with each other, at their borders, and exchange any surplus products they might have. In the third stage trade becomes regular and predictable: There is now production for exchange. The long-distance trade then reacts back upon the community itself, so that, in the fourth stage, an internal market is created. This stage is also marked by the emergence of money. The fifth stage, finally, is

---

4 It is tempting to see an ironical pattern in the recent tendencies toward market production in the communist countries: Would Marx have said that we are witnessing the third occurrence of the sequence?

characterized by production for surplus. It is defined not simply by the fact of exploitation but by the fact that the goal of exploitation is to increase the surplus, not just to consume it. In his Hegelian moments, Marx refers to this stage as the result of the self-expansion of money. To summarize: External trade changes production for immediate consumption into production for exchange; internal trade changes the latter into production for surplus.

This story commits Marx to the existence of production for surplus in the ancient world, when the sequence occurs for the first time. He occasionally refers to the transformation of a patriarchal slave economy into one based on the production for surplus. Elsewhere he insists, probably with more justification, on the obstacles that a slave economy creates for accumulation of surplus. With slaves it makes little sense to invest in improved means of production, because slaves can be expected to treat the tools badly; also, the psychology of slaveowners is such that they prefer luxury consumption to productive investment of the surplus. Another dubious implication of the scheme is the idea that external trade not only occurs before internal trade but is a direct cause of it. By and large, this does not seem to correspond to the historical experience. In antiquity, long-distance trade existed alongside local trade, but a national market was not formed. When it was, in the early modern period, it happened (as Marx also recognizes elsewhere) because of active state intervention, not as a more or less automatic consequence of foreign trade.

Also, as before, it remains a puzzle why the sequence had to occur twice. Marx raises the question of why capitalism based on wage labor did not develop in ancient Rome after the ruin of the small peasantry, but he does not really offer an explanation. The most plausible answer, perhaps, is that capitalism did not arise because there was no *competitive* national market. Slow transportation restricted exchange to local markets and international trade in a few luxury goods (and grain). If there had really been a fully developed internal market, to the extent suggested by Marx, capitalism would have been a more likely development. Nor does Marx explain why slavery gave rise to serfdom. Remarkably, he nowhere confronts the question of the breakdown of the ancient world. The general propositions of historical materialism imply, of course, that slavery disappeared when and because it became inferior to serfdom as a framework for developing the productive forces, but neither Marx nor any practicing Marxist historian to my knowledge has ever seriously considered this explanation.

It is clear that Marx thought that mankind as a whole could not have skipped any of the stages in either sequence. The modes of production had to follow each other in a specific order; the rise and fall of the market had to occur twice, each time through the same sequence of stages. It is less clear whether he thought that each country or nation-state had to go through the full sequence, or whether he admitted the possibility that some countries might enjoy "advantages of backwardness" and skip one or more stages. On the one hand, there is a passage in one of the prefaces to *Capital I* where he says that "the country that is more advanced industrially only shows, to the less developed, the image of its future." On the other hand, there is his suggestion, toward the end of his life, that Russia might be able to build communism directly on the basis of the communitarian village system without going through the capitalist Purgatory. Russia could employ the technology developed by the capitalist countries without itself having to follow in their steps.

The lesson from cases of successful or failed economic development in the last century seems to be that the position Marx took in *Capital* is the more plausible. If a country is too backward, it will not be able to make productive use of industrial technology. The rational utilization of borrowed technology requires a complex set of mental habits that cannot themselves be borrowed. They have to be developed from within. This need not require the same process that was followed by the advanced countries; indeed, the very existence of more developed countries creates a difference that makes simple repetition unlikely to succeed. Yet it is hard to deny that the more successful of the developing countries have followed the path of unbridled laissez-faire capitalism − a path that, presumably, will in time make it possible for them to dispense with that system. If there is any other path, no country has yet found it.

BIBLIOGRAPHY

*Introduction.* By far the best exposition of historical materialism is G. A. Cohen, *Karl Marx's Theory of History* (Oxford University Press, 1978), which supersedes all earlier treatments.

*The development of the productive forces.* Cohen's account of the explanatory role of the productive forces is usefully supplemented by P. van Parijs, "Marxism's central puzzle," in T. Ball and J. Farr (eds.), *After Marx* (Cambridge University Press, 1984), pp. 88–104. On the relation between development of the productive forces and population growth, see E. Boserup, *Population and Technological Change* (University of Chicago Press, 1981). For a controversial account of the transition to capitalism that emphasizes surplus extraction rather than technical change, see S. Marglin, "What do bosses do?" in A. Gorz (ed.), *The Division of Labour* (Longman, 1976), pp. 13–54. A very useful summary and discussion of Trotsky's views is B. Knei-Paz, *The Social and Political Thought of Leon Trotsky* (Oxford University Press, 1977). An influential discussion of the economic conditions for revolution is J. Davies, "Towards a theory of revolution," *American Sociological Review* 27 (1962): 1–19.

*Base and superstructure.* On this problem Cohen's book is supplemented by two of his later articles: "Reconsidering historical materialism," *Nomos* 26 (1983): 226–51, and "Restrictive and inclusive historical materialism," in B. Chavance (ed.), *Marx en Perspective* (Ecole des Hautes Etudes en Sciences Sociales, 1985), pp. 53–76. A challenge to the possibility of distinguishing base and superstructure in *any* society is S. Lukes, "Can the base be distinguished from the superstructure?" in D. Miller and L. Siedentorp (eds.), *The Nature of Political Theory* (Oxford University Press, 1983), pp. 103–20.

*The stages of historical development.* A good conceptual discussion of Marxist periodizations of history is E. Gellner, "A Russian Marxist philosophy of history," in E. Gellner (ed.), *Soviet and Western Anthropology* (Columbia University Press, 1980), pp. 54–82. Historiographic surveys of the difficulties met by Russian and Chinese communist historians in applying the Marxist theory of stages to their own countries include C. Black (ed.), *Rewriting Russian History* (Praeger, 1956), and A. Feuerwerker (ed.), *History in Communist China* (MIT Press, 1968). Discussions of the Russian dream – which is older than communism – of enjoying the advantages of backwardness and bypassing capitalism include A. Gerschenkron, *Economic Backwardness in Historical Perspective* (Harvard University Press, 1966), and Knei-Paz, *Social and Political Thought of Trotsky.*

# 7

# CLASS CONSCIOUSNESS AND CLASS STRUGGLE

IT is a truism that people have an interest in improving their situation. The strategies available to them are by individual and collective betterment. Let us focus on the respects in which their situation can only be collectively improved by the creation of public goods that are out of reach of individual effort. In any society there are organized groups trying to promote the interests, broadly conceived, of their members. There will also be many individuals who have strongly felt interests in some public good or collective action but for various reasons are unable to join forces with other people with similar interests. Finally, there will be some individuals who, objectively, would seem to have a strong interest in some public good, although, subjectively, they do not experience it that way.

Of these, the second group of people form an unstable category. If they are unable to rise into the first, they will tend to sink down to the third. In the long run, it is psychologically difficult to maintain a strong desire for something that manifestly is out of reach. The tension is usually resolved by reducing one's level of aspirations and adjusting one's set of values so as to give less importance to those that cannot be realized anyway. Occasionally it is also resolved by adjusting one's beliefs so as to be able to think it possible to get what one wants, but this solution is inherently less stable. Usually, sooner or later, the accumulation of evidence against one's belief will force a readjustment of wants and desires.

Marx's theory of class begins with a certain set of objectively defined interests, created by relations of exploitation and domination in production. Objectively speaking, people have an interest in not being exploited and dominated. For most of them, this interest can be realized only by collective action. Individual betterment by upward social mobility is an option for some but not for the great majority. The theory first addresses, albeit very scantily, the question of why some objective interests emerge as subjectively felt whereas others do not. It then investigates, much more extensively, people who have moved up from the third to the second category and then move farther up into the first. Taken together, these analyses amount to a theory of class consciousness.

Next, the theory addresses the problem of class struggle. When there are several organized classes with opposed interests, what will the outcome be of their confrontation with one another? Marx argued that this is the central problem in understanding social change, because he claimed that in the final analysis all social conflict reduces to class struggle. A crude version of this claim is that only class interests are capable of crystallizing into organized interest groups. In the light of the persisting importance of religious, ethnic, nationalistic, and linguistic social movements, the claim cannot be defended in this version. Other, more sophisticated versions also turn out to be invalid. Although the centrality of class struggle in social change cannot be defended as a general proposition, it was fairly plausible in Marx's time and place. His theory of class struggle in mid-nineteenth-century Europe remains one of his most impressive achievements, especially when taken together with, on the one hand, his theory of exploitation and, on the other, his theory of the capitalist state.

## THE CONCEPT OF CLASS

Marx never said in so many words what he meant by a class. It is nevertheless possible to reconstruct a definition from his writings by taking account of what groups he refers to as classes, what groups he explicitly says are not classes, and what purpose the concept is to serve in his wider theory. In particular, his view that classes are the basic units in social conflict requires a definition that yields a small, determinate, and nonarbitrary number of classes. Classes cannot be defined by arbitrary cut-off points on a continuous scale: They have real existence as organized interest groups, not just as constructs in the eye of the observer. On the other hand, class cannot be reduced to a dichotomous opposition between the haves and the have-nots, or the exploiters and the exploited. It is essential to Marx's approach that the number of classes, though small, must be greater than two, because otherwise there would be no room for the class alliances that play an important role in his theory of class struggle.

There are some fifteen groups that Marx refers to as classes: bureaucrats and theocrats in the Asiatic mode of production; freemen, slaves, plebeians, and patricians under slavery; lord, serf, guild master, and journeyman under feudalism; industrial capitalists, financial capitalists, landlords, peasantry, petty bourgeoisie, and wage laborers under capitalism. We cannot, however, simply define the concept of class by this list. To decide whether the examples form a coherent set, we need a general definition to check them against. Also, we want to be able to apply the concept to other societies than those studied by Marx. With respect to the societies he did study, we need to know whether his enumeration of classes is exhaustive or whether there could be others beyond those he cites. We must, in short, know by virtue of which properties these groups are classes.

One possible criterion can be excluded at the outset: Marx tells us in so many words that classes are not differentiated by income. Although members of different classes will, typically, earn different incomes, they need not do so; and, even when they do, it is not by virtue of this fact that they belong to different classes. He also rejects the idea that classes can be distinguished by the occupations of their members, that is, by the specific nature of the work they perform. The work context, not the work itself, is constitutive of class. Finally, we can exclude the idea that classes are differentiated by status, be it by the informal status criterion of honor or by the formal criterion of belonging to a legal order. Of these, the first yields a cultural and the second a juridical distinction; neither is an economic concept. Marx's reference to patricians and plebeians as distinct classes can only be seen as a lapse.[5] Although most of the

---

5 Another lapse in the list is the inclusion of freemen as a separate class. The notion is incomplete, as it does not specify the relation of the freeman to the other means of production, besides his own labor power. Once this is done, the catego-

plebeians were poor, some of them were indistinguishable from the patricians in all economic respects.

In contemporary social science, income, occupation, and status are the central concepts in the study of social stratification. This fact does not imply any inconsistency with Marxism, because stratification theory and class theory have different purposes. The latter addresses mainly the question of which organized *groups* will be the main actors in collective action and social conflict; the former, why *individuals* differ in such respects as deviance, consumption, health, or marriage habits. At least this distinction is valid with respect to Marx himself, who did not have a sociological theory in the modern sense of the term. In his dissection of capitalism the focus was almost exclusively on economic and political phenomena, at the expense of the texture and events of everyday life outside the work place. Later attempts to create a Marxist sociology based on the concept of class have addressed some of the same issues as stratification theory. To the extent that the concerns of the two approaches overlap, they are indeed incompatible, at least if each of them claims to provide the whole explanation of the phenomena under study.

Having rejected income, occupation, and status as criteria of class, four more plausible definitions must be considered: property, exploitation, market behavior, and domination. All have been seriously proposed by followers or scholars of Marx. With the exception of exploitation, all turn out to be necessary elements in the final, reconstructed definition. The task of reconstruction is difficult, because of the variety of economic systems to which the definition is to be applied. On the one hand, it must work equally well in market and nonmarket economies; on the other hand, it must be applicable both to societies in which the means of production are individually owned and to societies in which corporate ownership – by church, state, or the large modern corporation – is the rule. We begin with the case that most concerned Marx: market economies with individual ownership of the means of production.

ry subdivides into slaveowners, independent producers, and the propertyless free – three distinct classes rather than one.

Most frequently, class membership is defined by the ownership or lack of ownership of the means of production. For Marx's purpose, this definition cannot be the whole story, although it surely is an important part of it. Depending on how it is understood, it is either too coarse-grained or too fine-grained. It is too coarse if all agents who own some means of production beyond their own labor power are included in one class, because this would not allow us to distinguish landlord, capitalist, artisan, and peasant from each other. It is too fine if agents are relegated to different classes according to the quantity of means of production they own, because this would create an infinite fragmentation of classes. A similar objection can be raised to the use of exploitation as a criterion of class. If all exploiters are included in one class and all exploited in another, we fail to capture the subtleties of Marx's six-class model of capitalism. If, on the other hand, class becomes a matter of the degree of exploitation, the concept, once again, becomes too finely differentiated.

Market behavior is a more plausible criterion. The working class is made up of those who sell their labor power, the capitalist class by those who buy labor power; the petty bourgeoisie by those who do neither. The credit market, similarly, gives rise to the classes of lenders and borrowers of capital, and the pattern of land ownership creates the classes of landowners, tenants, and independent peasantry. The criterion, however, gives too much weight to actual behavior and insufficient weight to the causes of the behavior. A member of a rich family who takes a job as a factory worker to see what life is like at the bottom does not thereby become a member of the working class, nor does a self-proletarianized graduate student. Although they sell their labor power, they are not forced to do so. A worker is someone who sells his labor power because he has to or, more generally, because this is the best way he can use his productive endowments. The concept of class, to be useful in a theory of social struggle, ought only to group together those who are bound together, by necessity and a common fate. Hence, in market economies with private ownership of the means of production, a class consists of individuals who must engage in similar market behavior if they want to make the best use of what they have. Ownership of the means of production enters into this definition, not directly but as what determines which market behavior is optimal. *Endowment-generated behavior* becomes the criterion of class.

The criterion also applies, more obviously (and trivially), to nonmarket economies with individual ownership of the means of production. Slaves and serfs work for others because, given their lack of full property of their labor power, they cannot do better for themselves. Slaveowners and lords are surplus extractors because, given their ownership, in full or in part, of the labor power of others, this is their best strategy. The distribution of endowments generates the class structure in an immediate way. In market economies, the derivation is more indirect. One cannot predict, from mere inspection of who owns what, who will end up in which classes. A person who owns a little capital might, depending on the endowments of other agents, find that he can best make use of it as a worker, as a self-employed artisan, or as a small capitalist.

Economies with corporate ownership are more intractable. To understand their class structure, we must go beyond Marx in one important respect. Marx suggests that the ruling class in the Asiatic mode of production and similar systems consisted of the government officials who based their rule on exploitation of the peasantry. It is implausible, however, to think of the bureaucracy as a whole, from the emperor down to the doorman of his dining room, as one, unitary class. If the concept of class is to be of use in understanding social conflict, it must allow us to distinguish several classes within the bureaucracy. Exploitation does not provide a plausible dividing line. A subordinate bureaucrat would hardly be able to tell whether he received goods in excess of his labor time and, hence, would not know to which class he belonged. Class would become an analytical construct, not part of social reality. *Power* – relations of domination and subordination within a hierarchical chain of command – is more plausible as a differentiating criterion. One could distinguish, for example, among top managers, who only give orders; middle managers, who both receive and give orders; and subordinates, who are only at the receiving end of commands. Such relations are the stuff of social conflict; they are a natural extension of Marx's concept of class.

The same proposal immediately carries over to modern capitalism, dominated by large, hierarchically organized corporations. Given the objectives of Marx's theory, it would be absurd to make all employees of the corporation, from the president down to the unskilled worker, belong to the same class.[6] Again, the giving and receiving of commands seem to be the most plausible criterion for drawing internal lines of class division within the corporate hierarchy. The modern corporation rests on a triangular conflict of interests among shareholders, managers, and workers that differs in almost all important respects from the dichotomous conflict between capitalists and workers that concerned Marx.

Once again, however, the proposed criterion is too behavioral. We need to know by virtue of what assets some end up as top managers, others as middle managers, and still others, the majority, as simple subordinates. Skills probably count for much, as do various forms of "cultural capital" acquired in the family. These processes are still ill understood. The enormous salaries commanded by top executives also present a puzzle, beyond the general problems that skilled labor poses for Marxist theory. It is not clear why an executive vice-president is worth ten times as much to the firm as its chief engineer, even assuming that we knew why the latter earns five times as much as an unskilled worker. These problems point to the need for a Marxist theory of the firm that takes proper account of career structures and hierarchical domination.

It follows from this analysis that the immediate relations between classes are of two kinds. On the one hand, there is transfer of surplus from below; on the other, transfer of commands from above. Note that transfer of surplus is not the same as exploitation. Surplus is transferred from the capitalist tenant to the landowner, but the latter does not exploit the former. They are both exploiters, living off the labor of the workers they exploit. Similarly, there can be transfer of surplus from one exploited agent to another, as

6 If high executives receive stocks in the corporation on top of their salary, and thus become co-owners of it, the classical Marxist analysis remains to some extent applicable, but not without strain. When property is allocated as an incentive to performance, to reduce the "principal-agent problem" that otherwise plagues the large corporation, it can no longer be invoked as an independent variable explaining class position.

when an indebted artisan extracts a surplus from a few hired assistants and transfers it to his creditor while he himself remains, on the balance, exploited. Class conflict is, typically, caused by such immediate, face-to-face confrontations.

More remote relations may be more relevant. The assistants of the artisan ought perhaps to direct their struggle against the usurer who is exploiting their boss. The agricultural workers ought to see that behind their immediate enemy, the capitalist tenant, is a more formidable enemy, the landlord. Yet this is not the way the class struggle usually works. If anything, the remote enemy is seen as a potential alliance partner against the common opponent. This is even more clearly seen in hierarchical chains of command. There is a widespread tendency for the subjects in any bureaucratic society to direct their anger against the intermediate levels in the hierarchy and to absolve in advance the top level of any responsibility for their ills. "If only the king knew!" Because the class struggle often has this myopic character, it is perhaps less likely to bring about far-reaching social change than Marx believed.

## CLASS CONSCIOUSNESS

The concept of class, as defined, presupposes that there is interaction between members of different classes, by transfer of surplus or commands. It does not presuppose interaction among members of any given class or a consciousness of common interests. The theory of class consciousness attempts to explain under which conditions members of a class become aware that they have a common situation and interests and, moreover, are able to organize in a collective defense of those interests. Actually, the word "theory" is too strong. Marx offered some comments on the emergence of class consciousness among the English workers and the lack of it among the French peasantry. He also argued, albeit very ambiguously, that the capitalist state is an expression of capitalist class consciousness. These observations provide triangulation points for the construction of a more general theory of class consciousness, but they do not by themselves amount to such a theory.

In *The German Ideology* Marx puts his finger on the central obstacle to organized class action: the free-rider problem. "The attitude of the bourgeois to the institutions of his regime is like that of the Jew to the law; he evades them whenever it is possible to do so in each individual case, but he wants everybody else to observe them." Examples from Marx's writings include the regulation of the length of the working day, laws allowing expropriation of private property, and laws enforcing competition. He did not in equally explicit terms state the parallel dilemma for the working class, but it is obvious enough that strikes, trade union formation, and revolution also are subject to free-rider problems. *Explaining class consciousness amounts to explaining why members of a class choose the cooperative strategy in their Prisoner's Dilemma.*

Cooperation among class members can be studied in several perspectives. First, we may inquire into the proximate, subjective conditions for cooperation, that is, the information and the motivation that will induce class members to participate in collective action on behalf of their class. Next, we may search for the further, social conditions under which the requisite subjective conditions will be forthcoming. Or, finally, we may decide to short-circuit the subjective stage altogether and attempt to establish direct connections between social conditions and the propensity to cooperation. The first approach is that of the rational-choice theorist or the social psychologist, the last that of most historians or sociologists. The second represents an ideal synthesis, as difficult to achieve as it is rewarding. Marx, by and large, limited himself to the third, "black-box" approach. Although this may in some cases be an appropriate response to the risk of premature reductionism, it cannot in general claim superiority.

A first condition for concerted, collective action is that the members of the class have a correct understanding of their situation and their interest. The French peasantry around 1850, for instance, was under the sway of *idées napoléoniennes,* a conception of their interests that was adequate to the times of Napoleon I but no longer to those of his nephew, Napoleon III. The small landed property had corresponded to the interest of the peasantry when it represented a liberation from feudal oppression. It no longer did so when urban usurers had emerged as the new exploiters of the peasantry. Objectively, the peasants' interest now lay in an alliance with the urban proletariat, whereas before they had found a natural ally in the bourgeoisie. Subjectively, they were unable to go beyond the ancient, outdated conception of their interest.

Marx was somewhat more optimistic with respect to the capacity of English workers to form an adequate conception of their interests. Yet he was also frustrated by their lack of revolutionary class consciousness, which in part he imputed to their lack of understanding of their real interests. Around 1850, after the collapse of the Chartist movement, he explained their confusion by the fact that the workers were fighting a two-front war. Because the capitalists did not themselves take political power but left its exercise to the class of aristocratic landowners, the workers were confused about the nature of their real enemy – Capital or Government? Struggling simultaneously against political oppression and economic exploitation, and not understanding that the former was only the extension of the latter, they had a very diffuse notion of where their interest lay. Around 1870, the two-front war was replaced by an argument from divide-and-conquer. Marx suggests that had it not been for the presence of the Irish, the English workers would have been more able to perceive their real interest and their real enemy. Having someone below them to despise, they were distracted from the main enemy above them.

Marx's version of both arguments was excessively functionalist (or conspiratorial). He suggested that the presence of a government separate from capital and of internal cleavages in the working class could be explained by the fact that they provided a lightning rod to attract the anger of the workers and distract it from capital. The arguments can, however, be retained without appealing to this assumption. The second can be restated without any reference to the interests of capital and solely in terms of working-class psychology. The mental frustration and tension generated by a state of subordination are eased by drawing the main dividing line in society below rather than above oneself. In an echo of Rousseau's "Quiconque est maître ne peut être libre," Marx writes that "a people which subjugates another people forges its own chains." The first argument is a special case of the more general assertion that in a society with multiple, overlapping conflicts it may be hard to discern the main or ultimate cause of oppression (assuming, implausibly, that there is *one* ultimate cause that explains all the others). Another special case is the salience of face-to-face confrontations, as distinct from struggles against more remote opponents.

Assuming that the class members have a correct understanding of their interests as a class, what motivations are needed to generate collective action? Because Marx has little to offer by way of an answer, we are forced to go beyond the texts and offer some speculations based on recent work on collective action. On one account, which seems especially appropriate to capitalist collective action, cooperation is forthcoming because the members of a class engage in continuous or repeated interaction. They cooperate out of hope of reciprocation or fear of retaliation in later interactions. On another, which seems more adequate to working-class collective action, cooperation reflects a transformation of individual psychology so as to include feelings of solidarity, altruism, fairness, and the like. A related, yet different account suggests that collective action ceases to become a Prisoner's Dilemma because members cease to regard participation as costly: It becomes a benefit in itself, over and above the public good it is intended to produce. Finally, one ought not to exclude that collective action can occur because members act irrationally. This, however, is an explanation of last resort and should be invoked only when one can specify the kind of irrationality that is at work.

To choose among such explanations, one would need to know a great deal about the mental states of the individuals concerned, more, indeed, than is usually possible to glean from the historical record. Given the typical paucity of evidence, macrosociological correlations, explaining successful collective action in terms of social characteristics, are more robust. Marx emphasizes two such characteristics. On the one hand, the isolation or proximity of the members with respect to one another is an important factor in class consciousness. The impotence of the French peasantry, according to Marx, was due to their geographical isolation from each other and the lack of means of communication. Conversely, the greater class consciousness of the English factory workers is due to the fact that they are "disciplined, united, organized by the very mechanism of the process of capitalist production itself." On the other hand, although less centrally, Marx mentions high turnover in class membership as an obstacle to class consciousness. Like Tocqueville, Marx suggested that classes in America were in a state of "constant flux," which prevented them from solidifying into collective actors. Writing about Europe, he suggests that the small middle class is politically weak because it is "undergoing a constant process of decomposition and renewal."

There are other factors, less heavily stressed by Marx, that influence the probability of collective action. The standard of living, in absolute and relative terms, is particularly important. The absolute level shapes collective action in two, opposed ways. On the one hand, poverty offers a strong inducement to collective action, because the very poor have "nothing to lose but their chains" (unless the ruling classes make it their business to ensure that they face a fate worse than death if they fail). On the other hand, however, poverty creates an obstacle to collective action, which usually requires some resources. The very poorest workers may have the strongest inducement to strike but are also less able to go without the wage for a long time.[7] The net effect of these two tendencies is, in general, indeterminate.

The standard of living can also be assessed in relative terms, by comparison with that of other groups or with some expected level. Since Tocqueville, the following two propositions have been widely accepted. First, collective action is more likely to be generated by small inequalities than by large ones, because the latter are usually seen as immutable, quasinatural facts of the society in which one is living. Second, revolutions are more likely to occur when conditions have begun to improve than when they are stably bad, because expectations about further improvement tend to outrun the actual possibilities and thus to generate frustration.

The free-rider problems arising within the exploiting and dominating classes will, according to Marx, be solved by the state. This view will be discussed later. Whatever its plausibility as a theory of the state, it is obviously incomplete as a theory of collective action. For one thing, capitalists and other exploiting-dominating classes

---

7 Hence the slogan "Necessity is the mother of collective action" faces the same difficulty as the related idea that "Necessity is the mother of invention." The propositions could be tested by looking at the rate of union formation and of technical change during different stages of the trade cycle.

had problems of collective action before they achieved political power. For another, when there are several such classes in a given society, for example, landowners and capitalists, the state can at most enforce collective action for one of them, often at the expense of the others. For such nonstate solutions to collective action problems within the exploiting and dominating classes, we look in vain to Marx for guidance. He does not, for example, have anything to say about cartel formation, the capitalist analogue to trade union formation.

### CLASS STRUGGLE

The forms of class struggle are many and varied. They range from hidden manipulation to overt conflict; from direct confrontation between the two classes involved in a relation of exploitation or domination to complex alliance formation involving three or more classes. The interests of the parties may be implacably opposed or in concord in certain respects. The arena of class struggle can be an enterprise, a branch of the economy, or the political system; the stakes can range from wage increases to the creation of a wholly new set of relations of production. What makes a conflict into a class struggle is, first, that the parties involved are classes and, second, that the objects of the struggle are interests they have as classes, not as, say, citizens or ethnic groups.

Marx has little to say about class struggle in precapitalist societies, excepting a few remarks on classical antiquity. He observes that here the main form of class struggle was the conflict between debtors and creditors or small and large landowners. He explicitly says that the slaves took no part in the class struggle; rather, they were the "passive pedestal" of the class struggle between different groups of freemen. One can accept this view and yet argue that the objective conflict of interests between slaves and their owners was not without consequences. If there are few examples of slaves engaging in collective action, it is because slaveowners took care to reduce the likelihood of this happening by mixing slaves of different nationalities and in other ways manipulating the conditions under which slaves could become class-conscious.

Such *preemptive class struggle* is a very widespread phenomenon.

It includes, for instance, the deliberate choice of inferior technology if the best form would enhance the workers' class consciousness (by facilitating their communication with each other) or improve their bargaining leverage (by making them harder to replace or by making the firm more vulnerable to strikes that would let costly machinery lie idle). In contemporary capitalist societies it frequently takes the form of offering wage increases up to the level where the risk of trade union formation is eliminated but below the level that a union would be able to get for its members. In many societies class struggles have been preempted by the ruling class manipulating the means of communication, on the general principle of "divide and conquer." Sometimes these strategies are more efficient than violent repression of attempts by the exploited classes to organize themselves, because repression can have the effect of unifying the opposition rather than destroying it.

Marx was mainly concerned with overt forms of the class struggle, opposing two or more organized classes to each other. His analyses of mid-nineteenth-century class struggle in England, France, and Germany were, for the most part, based on the assumption of a triangular class constellation with, in addition to industrial capitalists and workers, a third force of landowners, financial capitalists, or government officials. Although Marx believed that the long-term outcome of the class struggle was shaped by the conflict between capital and labor, the modalities of struggle are strongly influenced by the presence of this third collective actor.

To the extent that the struggle between labor and capital concerns the very existence of the capitalist mode of production, they have diametrically opposed interests. Although Marx expected the class struggle to develop in this direction, the confrontation between capitalists and workers in his time had more immediate objects. Taking the capitalist organization of production for granted, workers demanded higher wages and better working conditions – as they do today. In this framework, capitalists and workers have some common interests. Although they have largely opposed interests about the division of the social product, both have an interest in increasing it. Hence, for instance, strikes and lockouts are double-edged weapons in the class struggle because of the loss of production they may cause. To some extent they also have overlapping interests about how the social pie is to be divided. Capitalists have an interest in restraining their short-term greed and avoiding overexploitation of the workers; workers have an interest in avoiding excessive wage claims, because future wage increases depend on something being left over for capitalist profit and reinvestment. Marx recognized these interdependencies of interest, although in his work they took second place to an assertion of conflict of interest.

Capitalists live off the surplus created by the workers. Marx insisted, however, that they also force the creation of the surplus they appropriate. In their entrepreneurial function, they are like brokers who bring people of complementary skills together, thereby making them more productive than they are in isolation. Although they have no right to appropriate the surplus they cause to be produced, it remains true that, in Marx's words, they "help create what is to be deducted." By contrast, he argued, landowners, financial capitalists, or bureaucrats do not even have this indirect productive function. They are nothing but parasites. Hence, there is a conflict that opposes workers and industrial capitalists, on the one hand, to the classes who make no contribution to the net social product, on the other. The two blocs are totally opposed, with no common interests.

Hence, on purely economic grounds, we would expect an alliance between workers and capitalists against these unproductive classes. This pattern of coalition formation was observed in the struggle of English capitalists and workers for the repeal of the Corn Laws or in the early stages of the French and German revolutions of 1848. Yet the capitalists soon find themselves in a dilemma: Having won with the help of the workers, they risk defeat at the hands of the workers. Referring to England, Marx writes that the capitalists then "prefer to compromise with the vanishing opponent rather than to strengthen the future enemy." In a near-contemporary comment on France, he asks, rhetorically: "The reduction of profit by finance, what is that compared with the abolition of profit by the proletariat?" There are two distinct reasons why the capitalist class might want to compromise with the precapitalist ruling classes, even at some cost to its profit. First, by combining their forces the exploiting classes can repress the exploited class more efficiently. This is the argument that Marx stresses in his writings on France and Germany. Second, there is the two-front-war argument: The capitalists can gain by blurring the lines of class conflict, that is, by forcing the workers to divide their energy between Capital and Government. This is the main argument cited in the writings on English politics.

This analysis rests on a divergence between the economic and the political interests of the capitalist class. This distinction is a special case of a more general one, between its short-term and long-term economic interests. The main long-term interest of capital is its long-term survival, which may depend on having a state whose decisions do not in each and every case coincide with the short-term economic interest of capital.[8] Recall here that the economic interests of the class can themselves diverge from the economic interests of each individual capitalist. These different ways of understanding *the* interest of capital add to the ambiguity and complexity of alliance formation.

Marx believed that the initial alliance between the productive classes against the unproductive ones was precarious, soon to be overturned by an alliance between the exploiting classes against the exploited one. Yet the coalition of the exploiters is only a holding operation. It can delay the historical trend, not reverse it. The inherent propensity of capitalism to generate exploitation, alienation, and various internal contradictions will ultimately sap its forces and lead to its abolition. When mechanisms immanent to capitalist production lead to a fall in the rate of profit, the capitalist class will have an overriding economic incentive to restore it by getting rid of the precapitalist parasites – but an equally strong political incentive to retain them. They are damned if they do but

8 In some cases the distinction between short-term and long-term economic interests has nothing to do with politics. Thus it may be in the short-term collective interest of the capitalist class to form cartels against foreign consumers, but its long-term viability may depend on vigorous competition and free trade, because otherwise foreign countries may be encouraged by the high cartel prices to develop their own industry. Here the interests of each individual capitalist coincide with the long-term interests of the class as a whole while diverging from the short-term collective interests.

equally damned if they don't. Marx summarizes their dilemma with a phrase from Juvenal: "Et propter vitam vivendi perdere causas" (for the sake of life to sacrifice life's only end).

In its main outlines, this view of history is badly, and irreparably, flawed. Marx offers no plausible story about how capitalism is doomed to destroy itself. Yet in small- and medium-sized details his theory of the class struggle in capitalism was an outstanding achievement. It would be wrong to say that it is a model of the genre, given the numerous ways in which the overall speculative views impinge on and distort the specific analyses. (This is particularly true of his analysis of the political dimension of the class struggle, to be discussed later.) Also, Marx's writings on the class struggle give us more than any careful model could ever do. They suggest numerous avenues of research, not all of them consistent with each other, yet each of them valuable and fruitful in some particular contexts. As always when reading Marx, one is struck by admiration for the brilliance of his intellect and dumbfounded by his lack of concern for consistency.

In Marx's vision of social change, class interests and class struggle were predominant. It may well be that in the mid-nineteenth century this view came closer to being true than ever before or since. Yet even at his time other causes and motivations, not immediately reducible to class interests, were important. In particular, what came to be known as "the national question" has been a stumbling block for Marxism since its inception. Workers and capitalists of oppressed countries rally around the cause of national liberation in a way that is hard to reconcile with the Marxist tenet that class solidarity overrides all other interests. Today, the "regional question" within capitalist countries poses a similar problem, as does the persistent and pervasive importance of racial, religious, and linguistic conflicts. One simply cannot defend the traditional Marxist view, that these nonclass interest groups will lose in importance as classes increasingly acquire class consciousness and organization.

Responding to this objection, Marxists have attempted to construct secondary lines of defense. One counterargument is that the nonclass interest groups owe their existence to class interests. Ethnic, cultural, or religious cleavages within the working class are explained by the fact that, by weakening the workers, they also benefit capitalist class interests. This functionalist account fails through a confusion of two phenomena classically distinguished by Georg Simmel in his sociology of conflict. On the one hand, there is *divide et impera*, in which the beneficiary actively creates and foments the conflict and distrust by which he maintains his rule. On the other hand, there is *tertius gaudens*, in which a third party benefits from a conflict he has not been instrumental in creating. Marx refers to the latter when he remarks that the workers' struggle for the Ten Hours Bill was favored by the conflict between industrialists and landowners, citing the English proverb that "When thieves fall out, honest men come into their own." It would be palpably absurd to assert that this conflict was engineered by the workers for their own purposes, yet a similar absurdity is committed by those who find capitalist intentions or benefits at work behind every conflict that opposes workers of different race or creed.

Another counterargument relies on a long historical perspective. It asserts that nonclass collective action may be important in the internal development of each mode of production but that class struggle is the decisive factor in the transition from one mode of production to another. New, optimal relations of production come about when and because their promotion coincides with the interest of a rising class, which is able, by virtue of this coincidence, to win out in the class struggle. The defect of this view is, again, its reliance on unsupported teleological thinking. No class gains the upper hand simply by being on the winning side of history. The conclusion seems inescapable that class struggle, though always an important part of social conflict and sometimes the most important part, is not always and everywhere its dominant form.

## BIBLIOGRAPHY

*Introduction.* The relation between individual and collective betterment has been brilliantly explored by three French writers: Alexis de Tocqueville in classical works on American democracy and the French Revolution; Paul Veyne in his book on authority relations in classical antiquity, *Le Pain et le Cirque* (Editions du Seuil, 1976); and Raymond Boudon in *The Unintended Consequences of Social Action* (St. Martin's Press, 1979).

## Class Consciousness and Class Struggle

*The concept of class.* The definition proposed here owes much to John Roemer, *A General Theory of Exploitation and Class* (Harvard University Press, 1982), and to G. A. Cohen, *Karl Marx's Theory of History* (Oxford University Press, 1978), pp. 70 ff. The importance of power for class formation in modern capitalist economies is stressed by Ralf Dahrendorf, *Class and Class Conflict in Industrial Society* (Routledge and Kegan Paul, 1957). An encyclopedic survey of Marx's writings on class is Hal Draper, *Karl Marx's Theory of Revolution,* vol. 2, *The Politics of Social Classes* (Monthly Review Press, 1978). A good account of social stratification theory is P. M. Blau and O. D. Duncan, *The American Occupational Structure* (Wiley, 1967).

*Class consciousness.* An outstanding historical study of class consciousness is E. P. Thompson, *The Making of the English Working Class* (Penguin, 1968). More dogmatic but also useful is John Foster, *Class Struggle and the Industrial Revolution* (Methuen, 1974). The relation between class consciousness and the collective action problem is discussed in Mancur Olson's classic book, *The Logic of Collective Action* (Harvard University Press, 1965). An application to capitalist collective action is John R. Bowman, "The logic of capitalist collective action," *Social Science Information* 21 (1982): 571–604. An application to collective action among the peasantry is Samuel Popkin, *The Rational Peasant* (University of California Press, 1979). There are not, to my knowledge, any good studies of working-class collective action in this perspective.

*Class struggle.* In addition to Thompson's book, the outstanding Marxist account of class struggle in history is G. E. M. de Ste. Croix, *The Class Struggle in the Ancient Greek World* (Duckworth, 1981). It includes, among other things, valuable discussions of preemptive class struggle, for which one may also consult R. B. Freeman and J. L. Medoff, *What Do Unions Do?* (Basic Books, 1984). A good study of class struggle in feudalism is Rodney Hilton, *Bond Men Made Free* (Methuen, 1973). Marx's accounts of social conflict in England, France, and Germany around 1850 may be usefully compared with, respectively, Harold Perkin, *The Origins of Modern English Society, 1780–1880* (Routledge and Kegan Paul, 1969), R. Rémond, *Les Droites en France* (Aubier, 1982), and T. S. Hamerow, *Restoration, Revolution, Reaction: Economics and Politics in Germany, 1815–1871* (Princeton University Press, 1966). The objection to Marxist class theory discussed toward the end has been most forcefully put by Frank Parkin, *Marxism and Class Theory* (Tavistock, 1979).

# 8

# MARX'S THEORY OF POLITICS

INTRODUCTION

THERE are two perspectives on politics in Marx's writings. On the one hand, politics is part of the superstructure and hence of the forces that oppose social change. The political system stabilizes the dominant economic relations. On the other hand, politics is a medium for revolution and hence for social change. New relations of production are ushered in by political struggles. To see the relation between the two functions of politics, they must be seen in the wider context of historical materialism. This theory affirms that new relations of production emerge when and because the existing ones cease to be optimal for the further development of the productive forces: This is the ultimate explanation of a change in the economic relations. In this transition, political struggle has no independent causal force. It acts as a midwife, bringing about what is doomed to come about sooner or later.

When the new relations have come about, the political movement that brought them into being is solidified into a political system that contributes to keeping them in place. When performing this stabilizing function, politics is initially progressive but later becomes reactionary. It is progressive as long as the relations of production remain optimal for the development of the productive forces; it becomes reactionary when new, superior relations appear at the horizon. In the latter stage, the political system can no longer be explained by its ability to stabilize economic relations, which themselves are further explained by their ability to promote the productive forces at an optimal rate. In its reactionary stage, the political system becomes an independent social force. It now keeps alive what formerly kept it alive, namely, a system of property rights that no longer can rest on its progressive economic function. It can only, however, give them a stay of execution. The political movement corresponding to the new relations of production will, inevitably, win out.

These general propositions are supposed to apply to all societies, from the Asiatic mode of production through slavery, serfdom, capitalism, up to communism. (There is one difference: The political movement that leads up to communism does not, after its victory, solidify into a new political system but rather proceeds to the dismantling of politics.) Actually, Marx and later Marxists have applied them to a much more limited set of problems: the rise and fall of capitalism. At the center of Marx's political writings is the capitalist state in its stabilizing function. He believed that he wrote at a time when the capitalist relations of production, from optimal, were turning suboptimal. Correspondingly, the capitalist state was in the process of going from its progressive to its reactionary stage. This is the overriding concern of his political theory: How does the state maintain and support capitalist relations of production in the face of the rise of communism as a potentially superior system?

He also made numerous brief observations on the political processes at both sides of capitalism: the political transition from feudalism to capitalism and from capitalism to communism. Though often suggestive, these are much less coherent than his theory of the capitalist state. They are also much less plausible, because they depend too heavily on the teleological framework of his theory of history. Marx never offers anything remotely resembling an argument for his view that individuals or classes will engage in political struggle for the sake of relations of production that will enable the productive forces to develop at an optimal rate. The extent to which he neglected microfoundations, and instead simply put his faith in history, is brought out in his irritation with the petty-minded German burghers during the 1848 movement, when they refused, contrary to the general movement of history, to enter into an alliance with the working class. Had he been more willing to entertain the idea that they were rational political actors instead of puppets of their historical destiny, he would have understood that if *he* could see that this alliance would ultimately

benefit the workers in their struggle against capitalism the burghers could also see what lay in store for them if they accepted it.

## THE CAPITALIST STATE

Marx had not one but two or three theories of the capitalist state.
Prior to 1848 he held a purely instrumental theory, usually
thought of as *the* Marxist theory of the state, according to which it
is "nothing but" a tool for the common interests of the bourgeoisie. After 1848, when this view became increasingly implausible, he substituted for it an "abdication theory," to the effect that
capitalists abstain from political power because they find their
interests better served this way. Finally, if one removes from the
second theory all that is sheer stipulation or unsubstantiated assertion, a more plausible account emerges. This is the view that the
state is an independent actor in the social arena and that the
interests of the capitalist class serve as constraints rather than goals
for its actions.

In *The Communist Manifesto* Marx tells us that "the executive of
the modern State is but a committee for managing the common
affairs of the whole bourgeoisie." In other pre-1848 writings he is
somewhat more careful. He recognizes that in most countries the
state is not yet fully capitalist in nature but adds that it must
inevitably become so if economic progress is to continue. "Bourgeois industry has reached a certain level when it must either win
an appropriate political system or perish"; by "appropriate" he
meant a system in which the bourgeoisie directly assumes the
political power. It was when Marx had to give up this basic premise that he developed the abdication theory of the state.

The instrumental theory has two sides to it. On the one hand,
the state solves the collective action problems of the bourgeoisie;
on the other hand, it blocks the cooperative solution to the similar
problems faced by the workers. Of these, the first task is more
fundamental and actually includes the second, because an unor-
ganized working class is a public good for the capitalists. In one
sense Marx stands in the Hobbesian tradition that views the state
as a means for enforcing cooperative behavior in a Prisoner's Dilemma. The crucial difference is that Hobbes thought of the relevant Prisoner's Dilemma as one involving the war of all against all,

whereas Marx restricted it to the internal war among members of the economically dominant class. In the only place where Marx refers to the function of the state in providing genuinely public goods, he adds that with the development of capitalism these will increasingly be provided by private industry. It is a puzzle why he should think that, say, basic research or defense against external enemies could profitably be undertaken by private firms; most probably he did not have a clear understanding of the problem.

Among the tasks of the capitalist state, Marx cites expropriation of private property when it is in the interest of the capitalist class as a whole; legal regulation of the length of the working day; and enforcement of competition. Of these, the last two are especially interesting. It is sometimes argued that the task of the state, rather than enforcing competition, is to save firms from the ravages of competition. If firms in an industry are unable to form a cartel, because of the free-rider problem involved, the state can force them to act in their collective interest. There have been quite a few instances of such forced cartelization in the history of capitalism, especially during the Great Depression. Marx argued that the state had to take the long view. In the long run, the viability and hence the legitimacy of capitalism depend upon the spur of competition. Similarly, he argued that the Ten Hours Bill of 1848 was introduced to protect capitalists against their short-term greed. By over-exploiting the workers, for the purpose of short-term profits, they were threatening the physical reproduction and survival of the class that formed the very condition for profit.

This argument presents a puzzle. If the state can act in the collective, long-term interests of the capitalist class, will it not also anticipate and prevent the communist revolution? Would not a state that does *not* say "Après nous le déluge" try to preempt any revolutionary social movement by reformist concessions? Marx did not confront this issue, except by a fiat to the effect that it would not arise, but on his behalf one might offer the following considerations. The natural response of ruling classes is to meet social unrest by repression rather than preemption. If it turns out that repression does not work, or has the very opposite effect of what was intended by unifying the forces it was supposed to crush, the rulers may turn to preemptive concessions as a fall-back strategy. In that case they will find, however, that preemption is a difficult technique to deploy. To be effective, it must be used before the demand for concessions has even arisen, because otherwise it will be taken as a sign of weakness and provoke still further demands. It remains true, nevertheless, that both repression and preemption sometimes do work. The principle that would guide a rational ruling class is either to give no concessions or to give more than is demanded.

Events in Europe between 1848 and 1852 showed that the bourgeoisie, far from reaching out toward political power, turned away from it. The English capitalists dismantled the successful Anti-Corn Law League, instead of using it as a stepping-stone to power. Having defeated the landowners over this particular issue, they showed no interest in dethroning them from power generally, to Marx's frustration and puzzlement. In France and Germany the revolutionary movement of 1848−9 was not the uninterrupted march forward of the bourgeoisie that Marx had predicted. Instead, it took the form "One step forward, two steps backward." The final outcome of the bourgeois struggle against feudal, absolutist, or bureaucratic regimes was not their dissolution but their further entrenchment. To remain consistent with his general theory of history, Marx had to argue that these noncapitalist regimes could ultimately be explained by the interests of the capitalist class.

This argument was provided by what I have called the abdication theory of the capitalist state, formulated by Marx in writings on French and English politics around 1852. ("Abdication" is used here in a somewhat extended sense, which includes abstaining from taking the power that is within one's reach as well as giving up the power that one has.) There are three steps in the argument. First, like several other writers, Marx argued that at this particular juncture in history the bourgeoisie benefited from having a state that was not the immediate extension of their interest. Next, unlike these other writers, he claimed that the existence of this noncapitalist state could actually be explained by these benefits. As usual, Marx had difficulties in accepting the idea that there can be accidental, nonexplanatory benefits in social life. Finally, he argued that, because the presence of a noncapitalist state could be explained by its value to the capitalist class, its autonomy was only an apparent one. This step is also questionable, because it neglects important strategic elements of the situation.

Many writers have been struck by the apparent paradox that England, the foremost capitalist country in the nineteenth century, was governed by a resolutely aristocratic elite, whose economic basis was ownership of land rather than capital. In earlier history, cumulation of economic and political superiority had almost invariably been the rule. The bourgeoisie was the first property-owning class that was not also the governing class. The most natural explanation of this fact, at least to a non-Marxist, is that the aristocracy had a traditional monopoly on government that was not easily broken. In the words of S. M. Lipset, the aristocracy "continued to maintain its control over the governmental machinery because it remained the highest status group in society." The alternative explanation, favored by Marx, is that the bourgeoisie shied away from power because it was not in their interest to take it.

Various writers have argued that the English bourgeoisie benefited from having a noncapitalist government. An editorial in the *Economist* from 1862, possibly written by Walter Bagehot, argued that "not only for the interest of the country at large, but especially for the interest of its commerce, it is in the highest degree desirable that the Government should stand high above the influence of commercial interest." The implication seems to be that a purely "commercial" or capitalist government would be too myopic or too greedy on behalf of capital, thus undermining its long-term interest. In a related argument Joseph Schumpeter claimed that the bourgeoisie "needs a master," not because they are too greedy but because they are too incompetent, "unable not only to lead the nation but even to take care of their particular class interests." In a quite different vein the English social historian G. D. H. Cole remarks that the English bourgeoisie "were too occupied with their own affairs to wish to take the exercise of political authority directly into their own hands."

The benefit cited by Marx was quite different. He argued that, were the capitalists to take political power, the two enemies of the working class – Capital and Government – would fuse into one, creating an explosive social situation. As long as the workers had to fight a two-front war, against economic exploitation and political oppression, their combativity and class consciousness would lack a clear focus. Recognizing this, the English bourgeoisie cleverly stayed away from power. Marx applied the same analysis to France. The revolution of 1848 led to the formation of the Second Republic and brought the bourgeoisie into political power. Yet they soon recognized that the July Monarchy (1830–48) had been a better arrangement from their point of view, "since they must now confront the subjugated classes and contend against them without mediation, without the concealment afforded by the crown." Hence, there was a need for a new blurring of the class lines, providentially ensured by Louis Napoleon. Marx interpreted Bonaparte's coup d'état of December 1851 as the abdication from power of the French bourgeoisie, just as he saw the dismantling of the Anti-Corn Law League as a deliberate stepping back from power by the English capitalists.

Marx, then, wanted to explain the presence of a noncapitalist state by the interests of the capitalist class. The explanation is not supported by the historical record. There is no evidence to suggest that the capitalists, individually or as a class, were motivated by such considerations. In the absence of subjective intentions, the objective benefits do not in themselves provide an explanation. Nor is it clear that the benefits cited by the *Economist* or by Schumpeter provide an explanation for the political passivity of the English bourgeoisie. A simpler explanation is provided by the logic of collective action. The free-rider problem ensures that capitalists will keep out of politics, unless intolerably provoked by state measures that go strongly against their interests. This fits in with Cole's argument: Although all capitalists would make more money if they all made some political effort, each individual capitalist would rather stay in business. It may then well be true that what capitalists do out of individual self-interest also, by a happy coincidence, benefits their class as a whole, but this fact is no part of the explanation of why they do it.

A variant of the argument can be applied to the French case, where the capitalists first had power and then lost it. Marx often suggests that the French bourgeoisie was weakened by internal dissensions among its several fractions and that this is what allowed Louis Bonaparte to take power. The observation suggests that the French bourgeoisie had not overcome their free-rider problems, that is, that they were not yet a stable collective actor. Hence they had little resistance to offer to the coup d'état. This fact, combined with the (alleged) benefits they derived from having a noncapitalist state, could be seen as justifying the view that they deliberately opted for the latter and abdicated from their own rule.

To see that the view is not justified, consider an analogy. A fugitive from justice may allow himself to be captured out of sheer exhaustion. It may turn out, moreover, that he does better for himself in prison than he would have done had he remained at liberty. These two facts, clearly, do not entitle us to say that he abdicated from liberty out of long-term self-interest or that the explanation of his being captured lies in the benefits he derived from being in prison. Writing about Germany, Marx does actually refer to the "Babylonian captivity" of the bourgeoisie in the decade following the 1849 counterrevolution, claiming that their lack of political power made them into the effective economic power in the land. In this case, however, he refrained from suggesting that their captivity was explained by those economic benefits.

Although there is little evidence for the view that capitalists abstained from power because they saw that this best served their interests, there could well be some truth in it. It could be that the lack of political ambitions on the part of individual capitalists was reinforced by the perception that even were they to overcome their free-rider problem they might not be well served by doing so. Evidence about individual motivations for abstaining from action is, by the nature of the case, hard to come by. Let us explore, therefore, the possibility that the benefits cited by the *Economist,* Schumpeter, and Marx did in fact enter into the explanation for the capitalist abstention from power. Marx claimed that if the presence of a noncapitalist state could be explained by such benefits it would prove that the state was "really" or ultimately a capitalist one. I shall argue against this view.

Marx held a narrow, *prestrategic* conception of power that prevented him from recognizing that the states he observed had autonomy in a real sense and not only as a fief from the capitalist class. To see this, observe first that there are two ways in which group interests can shape state policies: by serving as the goal those policies try to promote, or by serving as a constraint on them. On first glance, it is tempting to argue that if the choice between the feasible political alternatives is always made according to the interest of one group, then it has all power concentrated in its hands. On reflection, however, it is clear that power – real, as opposed to formal – must also include the ability to define the set of alternatives, to set constraints on what is feasible. The following scenario is intended to bring out the relations between these two ways of wielding power. It is constructed so as to apply to nineteenth-century European politics, as a strategic game between Capital and Government with the working class as an important background variable. In modified form, it could also apply to aspects of twentieth-century politics.

There are two agents: *A* (Capital) and *B* (Government), initially facing a given number of alternatives. *B* has the formal power to choose among the feasible alternatives; *A* may have the power to exclude some of the alternatives from being considered. We assume that in *A*'s judgment some alternatives are very bad, to be avoided at all costs. Among those remaining, some are judged better than others, but none is outstandingly superior. If the bad alternatives can somehow be excluded from the feasible set, it might not matter too much which of the remaining ones is chosen by *B*. It may not even be necessary for *A* to take any steps to exclude the inferior alternatives. *B*, acting on the "law of anticipated reactions," may abstain from choosing any of these, knowing that if he does *A* has the power and the motive to dethrone him. Moreover, to the extent that what is bad for *A* is also bad for *B*, perhaps because *B*'s affluence depends on that of *A*, *B* might not want to choose an inferior alternative even if he could get away with it. On the other hand, *A* might actually welcome the fact that *B* does not choose the alternative top-ranked by *A* – for example, if *A* does not want to be seen having power or if he deplores his own tendency to prefer short-term over long-term gains. Or, if he does not welcome it, he might at least tolerate it as the lesser evil, compared to the costs involved in *taking* the formal power (as distinct from the costs involved in *having* it). In either case *B* would be invested with some autonomous power of decision, although its substance might be questioned. Marx would say that the autonomy is only apparent, because ultimately it is granted by *A*. *B* has autonomy as a fief.

Consider, however, the same situation from *B*'s perspective. He will correctly perceive his power as deriving from the cost to *A* of having or taking it. To be sure, *B*'s power is limited by the fact that there are certain bounds that he cannot transgress without provoking *A* into taking power for himself, perhaps also by the need to avoid killing the goose that lays the golden eggs. But conversely, *A*'s real influence is limited by his desire not to assume formal, political power unless provoked. Both actors, in fact, have power, of an equally substantive character. How much power they have depends on the further, specific features of the situation, as may be seen by comparing cases *A* and *B* in Figure 1. (Needless to say, the following argument is extremely stylized; it is intended to be suggestive, not demonstrative.)

Each curve shows the amount of tax revenue to the state as a function of the tax rate. If the tax rate is 0, there is no tax income; if the tax rate is 100, no taxable activity will be forthcoming, and again there is no tax revenue. Somewhere in between there must be a tax rate, $t_{max}$, that maximizes government income. Let us assume, for simplicity, that this is the only interest of the govern-

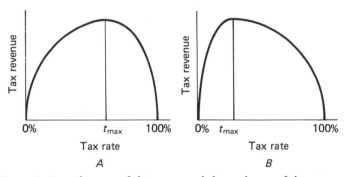

Figure 1. Two degrees of the structural dependence of the state on capital.

ment: to raise as much tax revenue as possible.[9] The interest of the capitalist class is, to simplify again, that the tax rate be as close to 0 as possible.[10] Depending on various economic factors, as well as on the form of tax collection, the optimal tax rate may be high, as in case *A*, or low, as in case *B*. In the former case, the government has substantial freedom to act against the interests of the capitalist class,[11] whereas in the latter it is constrained to track very closely what is optimal policy from the capitalist point of view. It is a purely empirical question whether, in any given case, something like case *A* or something like case *B* obtains.

We have seen some of the reasons why *A* might not want power. One is that *A* might know that if in power his decisions will be motivated by short-term gain to himself and that he wants to prevent this by letting the power remain safely outside his reach. From the point of view of *A*'s long-term interest, it may be better to have the decisions taken in accordance with *B*'s interest, although not, of course, as good as if *B* would take them to promote *A*'s long-term interest. Another reason could be the presence of a third actor, *C* (Labor), who is already opposed to *A* and who also tends to oppose whoever has the formal power of decision. For *A* it might then be better to leave the formal power with *B*, so that some of *C*'s attention and energy should be directed toward *B* and diverted from *A*. From this perspective, *A* might positively desire that *B* should not consistently decide in accordance with *A*'s long-term interest, because otherwise *C* might perceive that the distinction between *A* and *B* is quite spurious.

Finally, *A* has reasons for not wanting to take power, as distinct from his reasons for not having it. To go into politics is like a costly investment that bears fruit only after some time while requiring outlays in the present. If one's interests are reasonably well respected in the present, the prospect of a future in which they might

9 The government may also have an interest in a high growth rate for the economy, for instance if it believes that economic growth is necessary to stave off popular unrest.
10 The capitalist class may have a collective interest in some taxation, for the provision of public goods.
11 Assuming that the capitalist class is unable or unwilling to take power for itself – i.e., that there is no political constraint operating.

be even better respected need not be very attractive, considering the costs of transition. Myopia – a high evaluation of present as opposed to future income – might prevent A from wanting to take power, just as his knowledge of his own tendency to act myopically might prevent him from wanting to have it. These facts also create an incentive for B to make the transition costs as high as possible and to ensure that A's interest is just sufficiently respected to make them an effective deterrent.

In more concrete language, the state has an interest in maximizing tax revenue, the bourgeoisie in maximizing profits. How the state further uses its revenues does not concern us here. The substantive goals of the state can range from enriching the bureaucracy to promoting cultural expansion, imperialism, or social welfare. The fact that such activities are pursued by the state operating in a capitalist society does not prove that they are "really" in the interest of capital. Even if it is in the interest of capital to have a state with sufficient autonomy to pursue *some* such goals, the specific goals being pursued need not reflect that interest.

We saw above that if we consider only the economic constraint that the state faces – the need to keep alive the goose that lays the golden eggs – the government may have wide-ranging freedom to impose its interests on the capitalist class. These are not, however, the only relevant considerations. The goose need not just be kept alive; it should be healthy and thriving. The state has an interest in future tax revenue, not just in current income from taxation. If it maximizes income from taxes in the short run, there will be less left over for capitalist profit investment, and the creation of future taxable income. The state as well as the capitalist class can be the victim of myopia. There is, furthermore, a political constraint. If the state imposes a very high tax rate, which is optimal from the point of view of tax revenue, the capitalists might not sit still and take it. They have the resources and the motivation to overthrow the government if their interests are not sufficiently respected. Although the presence of a potentially dangerous working class may make them pull their punches for a while, they will not do so indefinitely. Knowing this, a rational government might not want to impose the tax rate that maximizes tax revenue. The binding constraint may be the political rather than the economic one. Fear for loss of power in the short run may accomplish what fear for loss of income in the long run does not.

Clearly, Marx underestimated the complexity of the situation he was discussing. The view that the English, French, and German governments had power simply as a fief from capital cannot be upheld. The basic flaw in Marx's analysis derives from a limited view of what constitutes a political resource. On his conception, power grows out of the end of a gun – or, more generally, out of money and manpower. Yet the power base of a political actor can also be his place in a web of strategic relationships. The capitalists' fear of the working class, for instance, gives a lever to the aristocratic government that has little to do with the physical resources it actually has at its disposal. Also, incumbent officeholders have an edge on their rivals that, again, does not derive from any prepolitical power base. Related phenomena in other domains are the general advantage of the defense over the offense in military matters and the disproportionate power that may accrue to a political party that happens to be in a pivotal position between the two major political blocs.

Marx argued that the presence of an autonomous, noncapitalist state could be explained by the structure of capitalist class interests. It is not clear that he was right. It is at least as plausible to explain the political abstention or abdication of the capitalists in terms of their individual interests. Even were he right, however, it does not follow that the autonomous policy decisions of the state can also be explained by these interests or that the autonomy was an illusory one. A state that can consistently impose policies very different from what capitalists would prefer and promote interests very different from theirs is a paradigm of autonomy. It does not become less so by the fact that the capitalist class may prefer this state over any feasible alternative.

## POLITICS IN THE TRANSITION TO CAPITALISM

Marx never wrote extensively about precapitalist politics. His views on the absolutist state and on the classical bourgeois revolutions must be reconstructed from a large number of brief texts, scattered around in his writings. The conception that emerges is surprisingly un-Marxist, in the sense that politics appears as anything but derivative. The decisive force in the shaping of modern history was not capitalism but the strong nation-states that emerged in the sixteenth and seventeenth centuries. For them, "plenty" was a means to "power" and subservient to power. The bourgeois revolutions of 1648 and 1789 brought the capitalists toward power but not all the way to power. Their rise was arrested, for the reasons set out above, and the state once again became a dominant, independent actor.

Unlike some recent Marxist historians, Marx did not argue that absolute monarchy was the political superstructure over feudalism. Perry Anderson writes, for example, that it was a "feudal monarchy" whose seeming "distance from the class from which it was recruited and whose interests it served" was in fact "the condition for its efficacy as a state." This amounts to saying that absolute monarchy was for the feudal aristocracy what in Marx's view the Bonapartist state was for the bourgeoisie – a tool, but at one remove. Marx did not, however, apply his theory of indirect class representation to the absolutist state. He argued that absolute monarchy was a competitor to the aristocracy and the bourgeoisie, not a tool, however indirectly, of either. In *The German Ideology* he refers to the period of absolutism as one in which "royal power, aristocracy and bourgeoisie are contending for domination and where, therefore, domination is shared." Elsewhere in the same work he suggests that the winner in this contest for the power was the state, at least in the early modern period. By mediating between the classes and playing them out against each other, the state could prevent either from getting the upper hand.

In *The German Ideology* Marx also asserts, without much argument, that the independence of the absolutist state was transitory and illusory. In later writings this view is spelled out in a more interesting way. Here he suggests that the independence of the state is self-defeating, because it cannot promote its interest without also strengthening one of its rivals, the bourgeoisie. The state does not stand in the same relation to the bourgeoisie as it does to the feudal nobility. The state and the nobility struggle over the division of a given surplus, created by the exploited peasantry. The state can gain only by reducing the power of the nobility. By contrast, the state will hurt its own economic interests if it interferes too much with the bourgeoisie, which is creating the "plenty" that the state needs to promote its "power." Up to a point the state will, out of its self-interest, further the interests of the bourgeoisie. By promoting the mobility of capital, labor, and goods and by creating a unified system of money, weights, and measures, the state allows the bourgeoisie to fill its own coffers as well as those of the state. The creation of competition and of a national market was not the quasiautomatic effect of foreign trade, as Marx suggests elsewhere. It required very deliberate state intervention against the numerous feudal barriers to mobility. Unlike the state in the Asiatic mode of production, the absolutist state actively reshapes the pattern of economic activities. Where it does not, as in Spain, Marx suggests that it is in fact to be ranged with Asiatic rather than European forms of government.

Beyond a certain point, this dependence on the bourgeoisie creates a dilemma for the state. If the state continues to encourage trade and industry, it will create a formidable internal rival. If it tries to hamper the bourgeoisie, it will reduce the economic and hence the military strength of the country, thereby laying it open to foreign rivals. (Marx does not actually make the last argument. The international dimension of absolutist policies is a major lacuna in his writings on the topic.) It would look, therefore, as if the state is in a fix: damned if it does and damned if it doesn't. What is strength with respect to the internal enemy is weakness with respect to the external, and vice versa. A balance may be found, but not easily. In particular, the attempts by many absolutist rulers to encourage industrialization without a general modernization of society have not been successful. Usually, they have got the worst of both worlds, not, as they hoped, the best of both. The equilibrium can be stabilized only by the emergence of an enemy of the internal enemy – by the rise of the working class that drives the bourgeoisie to ally itself with its former opponent against the new one.

What is the role, in this general picture, of the classical bourgeois revolutions? Almost all Marx has to say about the English revolution of 1640–88 is contained in a book review of Guizot's *Discours sur l'Histoire de la Révolution d'Angleterre,* which also offers a few comparisons with the French revolution of 1789. His numerous remarks on the French revolution are all very brief, except for a slightly more extended discussion in *The Holy Family.* Although the main characters and events of the French revolution were part of his mental universe and shaped the categories through which he interpreted current events, he never subjected it to a systematic analysis.

The two classical bourgeois revolutions had some features in common. They were transitions from absolute to constitutional monarchy, with a republican interlude. It would be misleading to focus on the transition from absolutism to republic as *the* revolution, because it is only the first stage in a process whose overall pattern is "Two steps forward, one step backward." In both revolutions this republican phase was accompanied by the formation of communist movements, who – following the revolutionary logic of going to extremes – wanted to take a third step. Marx suggests that the events of 1794, which he construed as a premature bid for power by the French proletariat, were part and parcel of the bourgeois revolution. There was a need to make a clean sweep of the past before the bourgeois order could be constructed. This historical task was, unbeknownst to themselves, performed by the workers. As usual, Marx could not resist the temptation to find a *meaning* in these aborted attempts.

The main difference between the two revolutions concerns the structure of the alliances that carried them out. "In 1648 the bourgeoisie was allied with the modern aristocracy against the monarchy, the feudal aristocracy and the established church. In 1789 the bourgeoisie was allied with the people against the monarchy, the aristocracy and the established church." Specifically, Marx suggests that the English revolution was carried out by an alliance of the bourgeoisie and the big landowners. The latter provided the former with the labor force it needed to operate its factories, while also benefiting from the general economic development that the bourgeoisie set in motion. The suggestion of a divided gentry appears to lack empirical support, and in any case the argument as a whole is a piece of blatantly anachronistic teleological thinking. In 1640 there were no actual or anticipated factories in need of workers. Also, Marx's characterization of the coalition structure behind the French revolution does not appear to stand up in the light of more recent research. French landed property was probably more integrated with bourgeois property than Marx thought.

Marx, however, thought that the explanation of the revolutions could be found in their achievements rather than in their causes. In an extravagantly teleological remark, he writes that the bourgeois revolutions "reflected the needs of the world at that time rather than the needs of those parts of the world where they occurred, that is England and France." The "needs of the world" amounted, essentially, to the abolition of feudal privilege and the creation of a regime of free competition. Whatever the revolutionaries may have thought they were doing, this is what they achieved.

This argument, however, presents a puzzle. On the one hand, Marx insisted on the progressive function of the absolute monarchies in creating a national market and abolishing barriers to competition. On the other hand, we now find him saying that these were the achievements of bourgeois revolutions directed against these very monarchies. The puzzle can be resolved by recalling the self-defeating character of absolutism. On the one hand, the absolutist state finds that it is in its interest as an autonomous agent to strengthen industry and hence the bourgeoisie. On the other hand, the protection of the material power of the bourgeoisie also tends to generate its political power and hence to threaten the autonomy of the state. The state, therefore, will be somewhat halfhearted in its defense of the bourgeois interests, trying, perhaps, to achieve industrialization without all the concomitant social and political reforms. At some point the state will want to stop further liberalization. At that point, however, the bourgeoisie may already be too strong to be stopped. If so, the bourgeois revolution will occur to complete the process begun by the absolute monarchy. Although a rational absolutist ruler might want to stop the process just before the bourgeoisie gathers the strength needed for a revolution, he is not likely to succeed in doing so, for three reasons. First, although we can, with the benefit of hindsight, perceive the internal tensions in the absolutist state, it is not clear that the absolutist rulers themselves were in a position to do so. Second, the need to fortify the country against external enemies may in any case have been more pressing. Third, depriving the bourgeoisie of the means to take political power would also deprive it of much of its economic usefulness. The only thing that will keep an economically vigorous bourgeoisie away from power is lack of motivation to take it.

Marx's analyses of the German revolution of 1848–9 can also be seen in this perspective. In the initial stage of the revolution he appears to have believed that the pattern of the French revolution would largely be reproduced. The alliance structure would be the same, except that the workers would play a more active part than merely carrying out the dirty work of the bourgeoisie, to be repressed as soon as their historical mission was fulfilled. Also, when the revolution made slower progress than expected, Marx put his trust in a repeat of the counterrevolutionary wars of the French revolution. Russia would intervene against Germany and ignite the revolutionary struggle.

Gradually, however, it dawned upon Marx that his adversaries could read the situation as well as he. If *he* could perceive that a bourgeois regime would set up conditions that, farther down the road, would undermine it, a rational bourgeoisie, reading the same signs, would keep away from power. If *he* could anticipate that Russian intervention would unleash the forces of revolution, a rational czar would remain passive. If *he* could learn from history, so could his adversaries. Marx sinned against a main rule of political rationality: Never make your plans strongly dependent on the assumption that the adversary is less than fully rational. (Because he tended to emphasize teleology rather than rationality, he rarely sinned against another: Never make your plans strongly dependent on the assumption that the adversary is fully rational.) Later communist leaders have been victims of the same hubris, most notably in the sequence of events that led up to the Shanghai massacre of Chinese communists in 1927. Although the CCP (or the Komintern) believed they could ally themselves with Chiang Kaishek for a while and discard him when his usefulness was exhausted, the manipulators ended up as the manipulated.

## POLITICS IN THE TRANSITION TO COMMUNISM

Marx's writings on the political transition to communism cluster in his two periods of intense political activity. Between 1848 and 1850 he wrote numerous political statements and newspaper articles from which one can glean some of his views on strategy and tactics. During the years of the First International, between 1865 and 1875, he also wrote widely on political and organizational matters. As evidence for his thinking, these texts are quite unreliable. Being shaped in large part by external, practical pressures, they reflect the spirit of compromise as well as sheer exhortation. Whereas circumstances biased the early texts toward what came to be known as ultraleftist deviation, the later probably reflect the opposite deviation. The radical artisans who formed the core of the Communist League and of the progressive faction of the 1848 movement wanted an immediate proletarian bid for power. Although Marx went along with some of their demands, he probably believed them to be utopian and premature. In his later years his public espousal of a possible peaceful road to communism may have represented a similar tactical concession. As a result, it is very difficult to reconstruct Marx's real views.

There are two central questions that ought to be faced by any theory of the communist revolution. First, under which conditions would a rational working class want to undertake a revolution? Second, how could a rational capitalist class or a rational government allow these conditions to arise? Failing plausible answers to these questions, a theory of revolution must invoke political irrationality on the part of workers, capitalists, or government. Marx, to be sure, did not state the problem in these terms. Nevertheless, because they seem to correspond to the reality of the situation, we must see whether his views can be restated within a framework of this type.

It follows from the central propositions of historical materialism that the communist revolution will occur *when* and *because* communist relations of production become optimal for the development of the productive forces. Let us first see whether this view can be defended and then examine the weaker versions that arise if we drop the causal or the chronological parts of the claim.

Marx argued that under capitalism the productive forces develop at an ever faster rate. Yet at some level of their development communist relations of production will allow for an even higher rate of their further progress. Hence, the communist revolution will be caused not by technical stagnation but by the prospect of an unprecedented technical expansion. The idea that communism will bypass capitalism with respect to the rate of innovation is itself highly implausible, but that is not our concern here. Rather, we must ask if this prospect can plausibly motivate the workers to carry out a revolution. Rational workers might, in the first place, be subject to a free-rider temptation that would block the efficacy of that motivation. Even if we assume that workers are able to act collectively to promote their common interests, a rational working class would still, in the second place, take account of the costs of transition and, moreover, be subject to some degree of myopia and risk aversion. It is not reasonable to expect workers to sacrifice what they have − a dynamic, efficient capitalism − for the sake of a remote and uncertain possibility of a system that will perform even better. Having much more to lose than their chains, they will be reluctant to throw them off.

A first retreat from this highy implausible view is to drop the causal implication of historical materialism while retaining the chronological one. On this view, what will motivate the workers to revolution is not the esoteric thought experiment that was just sketched. Rather, they will be driven to revolt because of directly observable features of capitalism: alienation, exploitation, waste, inefficiency, trade cycles. It just so happens that the time at which these ills become so grave as to create the subjective conditions for a communist revolution is also the time at which communism becomes objectively superior as a framework for developing the productive forces. The communist revolution occurs when but not because capitalism becomes a brake on further technical progress.

This view, too, is implausible. In Leon Trotsky's words, "societies are not so rational in building that the dates for proletarian dictatorship arrive exactly at that time when the economic and cultural conditions are ripe for socialism." Indeed, Trotsky's own work supports a stronger statement. Societies are systematically so irrational in building that the objective conditions for communism and the subjective conditions for a communist revolution never coincide. Theory suggests and experience confirms that communist revolutions will take place only in backward countries that are nowhere near the stage of development at which they could overtake capitalism. Russia around the turn of the century was a breeding ground for revolution because its backwardness created the proper economic and ideological conditions. Being a latecomer to economic development, Russian factories were free to employ techniques of large-scale production, requiring huge numbers of workers. Such concentration facilitates class consciousness, which is further helped by the absence of a reformist tradition and the possibility of drawing on the stock of advanced socialist ideas developed in the West.

For Marx's argument to be plausible, the ruling classes would have to be somewhat irrational. Because the development of the productive forces creates the material conditions for a general improvement in the standard of living, including protection against unemployment, he must assume that capitalists or government fail to deploy these means to preempt a communist revolution. Or, at the very least, he must assume that they deploy them irrationally and inefficiently, by combining stick and carrot in a way that only incites the revolutionary energy of the workers. Revolution is more likely to occur in a society where the level of development has not reached the stage where widespread concessions to the workers are affordable – but at that stage a communist revolution will also be premature, as far as the ability to develop the productive forces is concerned. These problems were at the root of the controversy between Mensheviks and Bolsheviks in the Russian socialist movement. The former wanted the workers to pull their punches in the struggle with the capitalists, so that capitalism could have the time to reach the stage at which a viable communism could be introduced. The latter argued, more realistically, that by postponing the revolution one would take it off the agenda for good.

Most of the time Marx seems to have assumed that the first communist revolution will occur in the most advanced capitalist country. In some writings, however, he anticipated Trotsky's "theory of combined and uneven development," according to which the center—periphery dimension of capitalism is crucial for the possibility of revolution. In *The Class Struggles in France* he wrote that although England is the "demiurge of the bourgeois cosmos" and the ultimate cause of capitalist crises, revolutions first occur on the European continent. "Violent outbreaks must naturally occur rather in the extremities of the bourgeois body than in its heart." Some thirty years later he suggested, in correspondence with Russian socialists, that Russia might enjoy "advantages of backwardness" that would allow it to bypass the capitalist stage and go directly on to communism.

This argument suggests that the subjective and the objective conditions for communism will be developed in different parts of the capitalist world system. The objective conditions emerge in the advanced capitalist countries, the subjective ones in the backward nations. How could the two sets of conditions be brought together? Around 1850 Marx argued, as did Trotsky after him, that revolution, once it had occurred in the capitalist periphery, would spread to the center. Again he put his hope in counterrevolutionary intervention as the mechanism that would ignite the general revolutionary conflagration; again he failed to see that a rational capitalist government would, for that very reason, abstain from intervening. Thirty years later he emphasized the diffusion of technology from West to East, rather than the diffusion of revolution in the opposite direction. This argument also fails, however, because it is much more difficult to borrow technology than Marx thought. The use of advanced industrial technology requires education and mental habits that cannot themselves be borrowed.

We must conclude, therefore, that Marx's theory of the communist revolution assumes that workers, capitalists, or governments of capitalist nations must behave irrationally. Because he did not provide any arguments for this assumption, his theory fails. The point is not that events could not conceivably develop according to one of these scenarios. Irrational behavior can be an extremely powerful political force. Rather, the point is that Marx provided no rational grounds for thinking that events would develop as he hoped. His scenarios were, essentially, based on wishful thinking, not on social analysis.

The socialist movement has entertained different conceptions of revolutionary strategy and tactics. They may be distinguished by the order in which the following goals are achieved: the proletarian seizure of power, the winning of a majority to the proletarian cause, and the transformation of society. According to one strategy, the workers should first seize power, then begin to change society, and finally win a majority. This was Lenin's strategy, using power to transform the peasantry into industrial workers who will adhere to the communist goals. There are indications that at one point Marx contemplated this strategy. Some of his statements on Germany after the bourgeoisie's retreat from power in December 1848 can support this "ultraleftist" conception but can also, with equal plausibility, be understood as compromise formulas. A variant of the minoritarian strategy is found in some comments on Russia from around 1870. Marx agrees that the Russian workers must take power while in a minority but adds that their first action must be to take measures to win the peasantry over to their side, thus effectively reversing the order of the last two stages in the Leninist strategy.

Another, reformist strategy proposes to begin by transforming society from within, thus creating a majority for communism that will make the final seizure of power a mere formality. Again, there is some support for this view in Marx's writings. In *Capital III* he describes how joint-stock companies and workers' cooperatives effectuate "the abolition of the capitalist mode of production within the capitalist mode of production itself." We should not infer, however, that he believed this could be the main road to communism. This is pretty obvious with respect to joint-stock companies, but the case for workers' cooperatives might seem more promising. The obstacle to this path, however, is that communist enclaves within capitalism will function badly precisely because they operate within a hostile environment; reforms that are viable in the large may work badly when implemented in the small. "Restricted to the dwarfish forms into which individual wage slaves can elaborate it by their private efforts, the cooperative system will never transform capitalistic society."

Finally, there is the strategy of the majority revolution in which the workers win a majority, seize power, and use it to change society. This was certainly Marx's preferred strategy with respect to the advanced capitalist countries, which remained crucial to the prospect of revolution, even if it were to start as a minority movement in the backward countries. The further modalities of the majority revolution depend on the answers given to three interrelated questions. Was the working class to organize itself secretly or openly? Should it use the existing political institutions or work outside them? Would it be possible to introduce communism by peaceful measures, or would a violent revolution prove necessary?

On the first issue Marx's position was perfectly clear. He was consistently opposed to secret societies and conspiracies, arguing that "if the working classes conspire, they conspire publicly, as the sun conspires against darkness." On the other issues his views were more nuanced. Writing about France and Germany, he argued that it would be disastrous if the workers tried to use the existing state apparatus to further their own purposes. Some articles on England suggest a similar view. He argued that the political opposition was mainly useful to the government as a safety valve: "it does not stop the motion of the engine, but preserves it by letting off in *vapour* the power which might otherwise blow up the whole concern." Yet with the rise of Bakunin's faction in the International, he felt the need to demarcate himself from the anarchists on his left, not merely from the state socialists on his right. In an article on "political indifferentism" he warns against the idea that any involvement with the state is contrary to the interests of the workers, citing the English Factory Acts as an example of what can be achieved by working within the existing institutions.

In *The German Ideology* Marx made a point that was later to be developed by the French socialist Sorel (much admired by Mussolini). A violent revolution is doubly necessary, "not only because the *ruling* class cannot be overthrown in any other way, but also because the class *overthrowing* it can only in a revolution succeed in ridding itself of all the muck of ages and become fitted to found society anew." His later writings moved away from this view, emphasizing that a peaceful transition was desirable and arguably also possible. In 1852 Marx asserted that the inevitable result of universal suffrage in England would be the political supremacy of the working class, suggesting the possibility of a peaceful road to communism. In speeches and interviews around 1870 he suggests that this path, although blocked in countries with a history of violent repression of the workers such as France, may be feasible in England and Holland where the political traditions are different. It is difficult to decide whether these were statements made on the grounds of political expediency or whether they correspond to deeply held convictions.

Between the communist revolution and the full-blown communist society there lie two intermediate forms. The first is "the dictatorship of the proletariat," a phrase that has acquired an ominous meaning that probably was not present to Marx and his contemporaries. Dictatorship at his time and in his work did not necessarily mean anything incompatible with democracy. Rather, it involves a form of extralegality, a political rule in breach of the existing constitution. From *The Civil War in France,* where Marx considers the Paris Commune as a model of the dictatorship of the proletariat, we can infer that it also involves majority rule, dismantling of the existing state apparatus, and instant revocability of the political representatives of the people. In one text there is a brief reference to "crushing the resistance of the bourgeoisie," but again we should not assume that the phrase must be read with the sinister meaning that comes most easily to the contemporary reader.

The dictatorship of the proletariat is a stage in the political transition to communism. In the *Critique of the Gotha Program* Marx states that it is succeeded by an economic transitional form, which Marx refers to as the lower stage of communism. Roughly speaking, it is a form of state socialism with distribution according to labor effort. Marx has very little to say about these two intermediate stages and their relation to one another. Perhaps he could be read as suggesting that the dictatorship of the proletariat is necessary because of the conflicts of interest that will exist between workers and the former capitalists, whereas the institutions in the lower stage of communism are necessitated by the conflict of interest among the workers, who will still be imbued with capitalist mentality even though the capitalist class has disappeared.

In the final stage of communism, all political institutions disappear. What takes their place is the self-government of the community – a task, according to Marx, no more difficult than the control of an individual over himself. With the disappearance of alienation and exploitation, social relations will be perfectly transparent and nonconflictual. This conception of communism is massively utopian. Social causality will always to some extent remain opaque. There are many other grounds for conflict of interest besides exploitation: Even in communism people will disagree over protection of the environment, the rights of the unborn or of future generations, the proper amount of the social product to be spent on health care, and similar issues.

Ultimately, Marx's vision of the good society was of organic character. He conceived of communism as a society of individual producers in spontaneous coordination, much as the cells of the body work together for the common good – with the difference that Marx insisted on the uniqueness of each individual producer. No such society will ever exist; to believe it will is to court disaster.

BIBLIOGRAPHY

*Introduction.* An encyclopedic survey of Marx's political writings is Hal Draper, *Karl Marx's Theory of Revolution,* vol. 1, *State and Bureaucracy* (Monthly Review Press, 1977). A valuable conceptual discussion is J. Maguire, *Marx's Theory of Politics* (Cambridge University Press, 1978).

*The capitalist state.* The view that the task of the state is to enforce the cooperative solution to a Prisoner's Dilemma is argued in M. Taylor, *Anarchy and Cooperation* (Wiley, 1976). Interpretations of the noncoincidence of economic and political power in capitalism include S. M. Lipset, "Social stratification: social class," in *International Encyclopedia of the Social Sciences* (Macmillan, 1968), vol. 15; J. Schumpeter, *Capitalism, Socialism, and Democracy* (Allen and Unwin, 1961); G. D. H. Cole, *Studies in Class Structure* (Routledge and Kegan Paul, 1955). The argument for state autonomy made here owes much to D. North, *Structure and Change in Economic History* (Norton, 1981), and to the essays by A. Przeworski collected in his *Capitalism and Social Democracy* (Cambridge University Press, 1985).

*Politics in the transition to capitalism.* The contrast between "plenty" and "power" is taken from J. Viner, "Power versus plenty as objectives of foreign policy in the seventeenth and eighteenth centuries," *World Politics* 1 (1948): 1–29. Recent Marxist studies of absolutism include P. Anderson, *Lineages of the Absolutist State* (New Left Books, 1974), and R. Brenner, "The agrarian roots of European capitalism," *Past and Present* 97 (1982): 16–113. A brilliant brief account of the English revolution is L.

# Bibliography

Stone, *The Causes of the English Revolution, 1529–1642* (Routledge and Kegan Paul, 1972). Among the many works on the French revolution, two books by F. Furet are especially relevant in the present perspective: *Penser la Révolution Française* (Gallimard, 1978) and *Marx et la Révolution Française* (forthcoming). Marx's articles on and during the German revolution may be usefully read with T. S. Hamerow, *Restoration, Revolution, Reaction: Economics and Politics in Germany, 1815–1871* (Princeton University Press, 1966).

*Politics in the transition to communism.* A good introduction to the rationality of revolutionary behavior is J. Roemer, "Rationalizing revolutionary ideology," *Econometrica* 53 (1985): 84–108. The prospects for communism in backward countries are discussed in L. Trotsky, *A History of the Russian Revolution* (Pluto Press, 1977), and in B. Knei-Paz, *The Social and Political Thought of Leon Trotsky* (Oxford University Press, 1977). Marx's political thinking before 1850 is exhaustively documented and discussed in R. Hunt, *The Political Ideas of Marx and Engels,* vol. 1, *Marxism and Totalitarian Democracy, 1818–1850* (University of Pittsburgh Press, 1974). The discussion of the various revolutionary strategies draws heavily on S. Moore, *Three Tactics* (Monthly Review Press, 1963). Another valuable book by the same author is *Marx on the Choice between Socialism and Communism* (Harvard University Press, 1980).

# 9

# THE MARXIST CRITIQUE OF IDEOLOGY

INTRODUCTION

$\mathbf{M}$ARX'S critique of ideology has been among the most influential of his ideas. Marx, Nietzsche, and Freud are currently seen as the great debunkers, who taught us never to take words at their face value but always to look behind them for some psychological or social interest they express or some situation that unbeknownst to the agents shape their thoughts and desires. When we refer to a view as an instance of *false consciousness* – a frequently used term for ideological thinking – we do not simply label it as an error or misperception, a thought that is false to the facts. We suggest that it is falsified and distorted in a systematic way, by causal processes that impede the search for truth. Unlike an accidental mistake, which offers little resistance to correction (beyond the general reluctance to admit error), ideologies are shaped by deep-seated tendencies that help them survive criticism and refutation for a long time.

What are the forces that shape and maintain ideological thinking? The standard and, as it were, official Marxist answer is *interest;* more specifically, the interest of the ruling class. On this point Marxism deviates from the Freudian conception of false consciousness, according to which it is necessarily the interest of the person himself that distorts his thinking, not that of some other person or class. The central question, which is usually left unresolved by Marxist writers on ideology (including Marx), is *how* – by what mechanism – the interest of the ruling class is supposed to shape the views of other members of society. The view that rulers and exploiters shape the world view of the oppressed by conscious, cynical manipulation is too simplistic, not because there have been no attempts to do exactly this but because they are

168

unlikely to succeed. By and large, cynicism in the rulers breeds cynicism, not belief, among the subjects. Conversely, successful indoctrination requires that the rulers believe in what they are preaching; they must not have a purely instrumental attitude toward their doctrines. Needless to say, the mere fact that a ruling class benefits from the illusions of their subjects does not prove that it is causally responsible for them. If, for some reason or other, the subjects fall victim to ideological misrepresentation of the world, this is likely to harm their interests and, to that extent, to benefit the rulers even if the latter were in no way causally involved in the error.

Marx does not, however, always stick to his official answer. He also suggests that ideologies can arise or take root spontaneously in the minds of those subject to them, without any assistance from others. Here, again, he differs from the Freudian conception of false consciousness by stressing the social causation of ideology rather than any individualized genetic account. Ideology in Marx's sense is not an idiosyncratic complex of beliefs and attitudes caused by a unique set of experiences. It is a figure of thought shared by many people and caused by whatever is common in their situation. Although psychoanalysis may well address itself to the exceptional, as in Freud's study of Leonardo da Vinci, the Marxist critique of ideology must look at what is typical, widespread, mediocre.

There is another difference between Freud's psychological and Marx's sociological conception of false consciousness. According to psychoanalytic theory, the object of individual attitudes is the individual himself – his experiences, his perception of other people, including his perception of their perception of him. With some exceptions, psychoanalytical theory does not try to explain people's political attitudes or their views on social causality. The Marxist theory of ideology addresses itself to factual and normative beliefs about society.[12] This difference is connected to an-

12 To be sure, there have been attempts to explain, say, physical theories as ideological constructions. By and large, however, they have been spectacularly unsuccessful. They have usually rested on arbitrarily selected "similarities" between features of a physical theory and features of society, without any attempt to produce evidence for a causal connection.

other. In Freudian theory one usually assumes that the false consciousness is accompanied by an unconscious awareness of the true state of affairs – an awareness that the person has repressed, substituting for it a false representation. False consciousness involves self-deception. The Marxist theory of ideology makes no similar assumption. True, in the formation of ideology there is often (but far from always) an element of wishful thinking, the belief that the world is as one would like it to be, but this phenomenon differs from self-deception in that there is no dual belief system at work. The assumption of self-deception in Freudian theory appears plausible because the person stands in a peculiarly intimate relation to the true facts about himself; it might look as if in some sense he can hardly avoid knowing them. Whatever one thinks of this argument, there is no way in which people have immediate access to the truth about society. Any view of society – true or false, distorted or not – is a construction.

Shared ideological beliefs arise in two ways. They can emerge simultaneously and spontaneously in the minds of many people, who are exposed to similar external influences and subject to similar psychological processes. Or they arise first in the mind of one person and then spread by diffusion to other people who for some reason are disposed to accept them. The sociology of knowledge – the non-Marxist version of the theory of ideology – makes a useful distinction between the study of the production of ideas and the study of the acceptation of ideas. To use a biological analogy, one may hold that ideas appear like mutations, at random, and then become rejected or accepted according to their "social fitness."[13] Or one may hold that the emergence of ideas is itself a phenomenon that can be studied sociologically. Ideas that are "in the air" may appear simultaneously in several places.[14] The Marxist theory of ideologies employs both methods.

13 The analogy, as usual in such cases, has only partial validity, because different people can accept different ideas, corresponding to their social position and interest. One cannot expect a dominant ideology to emerge by chance variation and social selection, in the way features of organisms develop by chance variation and natural selection.

14 There are various further possibilities. One might argue that social conditions, though neutral with respect to the content of new ideas, can speed up or slow down the rate at which they appear. Or one might argue that social conditions,

There are two kinds of attitudes that are subject to ideological bias: affective and cognitive, or "hot" and "cold." What people value for themselves, what they believe is morally required of themselves and others, how they think society's goods ought to be distributed – these are matters that directly engage their passions. What they believe with respect to particular issues of fact and general causal connections are not matters that in themselves engage their passion, except possibly the passion for truth. A rational person would try to arrive at these factual beliefs in a coolly detached way, because beliefs formed in these ways have a better chance of being true and because true beliefs have a better chance of serving his passions than false beliefs. Recall Paul Veyne's phrase: Beliefs shaped by passion serve passion badly.

The bias that shapes ideological attitudes can itself be affective or cognitive, hot or cold. Hence, we may distinguish among four kinds of ideological attitudes, according to whether the attitudes themselves and the biases underlying them are hot or cold. First, affective attitudes may be shaped by affectively biased processes, as in the story of the fox and the grapes. People often adjust their aspirations to what seems feasible, so as to avoid living with the tension and frustration caused by the desire for the unattainable. Second, and perhaps surprisingly, hot motivations may be shaped by cold cognitive factors, as when preferences are reversed by redescribing the options.[15] Third, cognitive attitudes are often shaped by motivational processes, as in the phenomena of wishful thinking, self-deception, and the like. Finally, cognition may be subject to specifically cognitive distortions, as when people have too much confidence in small samples or otherwise ignore the basic principles of statistical inference.

Of these mechanisms, all but the second have some importance in Marx's theory of ideology. The first underlies his often cited statement that religion is the "opium of the people," with the concomitant idea that religion helps people adapt to their miserable lives in this world. The third operates in the selection of world

though not uniquely determining what will appear, set limits on the content of new ideas.
15 People who will not use credit cards if they incur a surcharge for using them may not mind doing so if there is a cash discount.

views: Among the many different accounts of social and economic causation, each group or class will select one that seems to justify special consideration for its interests. The last is important when Marx offers *class position* rather than *class interest* as the source of ideological thinking. The third mechanism and the fourth are somewhat similar in that both can be characterized as *pars pro toto* fallacies. Ideology formation by wishful thinking operates when members or representatives of a particular class stipulate that the realization of their interest coincides with the realization of the interests of society as a whole. Ideology formation by class-specific illusions operates when members of a particular class believe that the causal processes they can observe from their particular standpoint also are valid for the economy as a whole.

Hence, Marx's actual studies of ideological thought differ from his "official theory" – the ruling ideas are the ideas that serve the interest of the ruling class – in two ways. First, when he refers to interest as an explanation of ideology, it is often in a causal rather than a functional mode. Instead of pointing to the consequences of a certain belief with respect to certain interests, he cites the interest as the cause of the belief. One cannot conclude that interest-generated beliefs will serve the interest of the believer, because "beliefs shaped by passion serve passion badly," or that it will serve the interest of the ruling class, because some of the beliefs of that class may themselves be shaped by interest. Second, class position as well as class interest enters into the explanation of ideological thinking. Again, such class-based illusions will not tend to serve the interest of class members or the interests of the ruling class if its members are also victims of this mechanism.

Ideologies belong to the superstructure, defined as the set of noneconomic phenomena in society that can be explained by the economic structure. The argument in the preceding paragraph was directed against the view that all superstructural phenomena tend to stabilize the economic structure by serving the interest of the ruling class; and, by implication, against the idea that the superstructure can be explained by its tendency to stabilize the economic structure. Even, however, when beliefs serve the interest of the rulers, this need not be part of the explanation of why they are held. If the subjects, to reduce cognitive dissonance, limit their aspiration level to what is feasible so that, for instance, they have no desire for political freedom, this clearly serves the interest of the rulers. Yet the explanation in this case will be found in the interest and needs of the subjects.[16]

## POLITICAL IDEOLOGIES

In *The German Ideology* and in the political writings on France, Marx elaborated a theory of political ideology that, although somewhat obscure and hard to grasp in its details, remains valuable and useful in broad outlines. The central argument concerns the relation between the special interests of a given class and the general interests of society. Two questions are involved. First, what is the causal role of particular class interests in shaping the class members' conceptions of the general interest? Second, to what extent does the realization of particular interests coincide with the realization of the general interest? Class members, or at least their ideological representatives, always think that the general interest can best be realized by measures that also happen to promote their special interests. Sometimes this belief is in fact true, or at least accepted as true by members of other classes. When this is the case, the class in question acquires irresistible force and momentum, as was true of the French bourgeoisie in the events leading up to 1789. Its demand for the abolition of privileges struck a profound chord in other parts of the population. When it is not the case, the class appears as hopelessly utopian and impotent, as was the case of the French petty bourgeoisie in 1848. Its demand for cheap credit was not seen as corresponding to anyone else's interest.

According to this view, a political ideology is not a pure expression of self-interest. Political struggle is not a form of bargaining, in which self-interest is recognized as the motivating force of all participants. As noted by Tocqueville around 1830, political parties that are too manifestly motivated by self-interest will not

16 Whether the need for dissonance reduction corresponds to the real interest of the subjects, in the sense of an objective interest in liberation from oppression, is irrevelant here. To have explanatory power, an interest must be *actual*; whether it is also *real* in some objective sense cannot make a difference.

inflame their audience or, more importantly, their own members; "ils s'échauffent toujours à froid." At the very least, one has to pretend to act for the general interest. When working-class parties demand redistribution of income in their favor, they usually feel an obligation to argue that it will not cause massive damage to economic efficiency.[17] When their opponents demand tax cuts, they usually add that trickle-down benefits and supply-side effects will work out in the interest of all.

More strongly, one can argue that class members or representatives will actually believe or come to believe in the identity of their special interest and the general interest. Three arguments point in this direction. First, one can invoke a natural-selection argument: Parties with leaders who do not believe in their own ideology will fail to carry conviction and gain adherents. Second, there is a psychological argument: Even people who initially are just pretending to argue in terms of the general interest will, after some time, come to believe in what they are saying. Third, it is by no means difficult to acquire the conviction that the general interest is served by implementing one's own particular interest; the nature of social reality and of the human psyche conspire to make it very easy indeed. Let me expand on the third point, which is of fundamental importance.

For one thing, it is frequently true that there are several institutional arrangements, all of which are better for everyone than a state of anarchy and each of which has the additional effect of selectively favoring the interests of a particular class. By comparing the effect of a given policy with the effect of having no policy at all rather than with the effect of another policy, it is easy to represent it as being in everybody's interest. For another, given the complexity of social causation and interaction, there is rarely full agreement among social scientists, and often there is strong and persistent

---

17 For instance, it is not likely that any political party would explicitly advocate the distributive solution argued by John Rawls, that income ought to be distributed so as to maximize the welfare of the worst-off group of people in society. At the very least, this advocacy would be politically suicidal if the last small increment of welfare of that group could be achieved only by a large reduction in the welfare of everybody else.

disagreement. Among contending views on social causation, and notably among contending economic theories, it is often possible to find one that asserts or implies that implementing the particular interest of one class is the *only* way of promoting the common good. In that case, nothing is more human than to espouse that theory as the correct account of how the world works and to argue in good faith that everyone will be better off by removing all obstacles to the realization of the particular set of interests that just happen to be one's own. On this account, the impact of special interests on specific policy options is mediated by a conception of the general interest.[18] Because the connection is indirect rather than immediate, it need not obtain in each and every case. Up to a certain point, this is all to the benefit of the class, because its claim to represent the general interest is more credible if it occasionally advocates policies that go against its particular interests. This does not, of course, carry any implication that this benefit *explains* why a class sometimes espouses such policies.

A political movement, on this account, is a *standing offer* to the public. The offer is taken up when circumstances are such as to make it appear favorable. It is a bit like a broken-down watch that shows the correct time once in every twelve hours. In a capitalist economy there will always be some parties advocating more central planning, others arguing for an extension of the welfare state, and still others for giving freer rein to market forces, all on the grounds of the common good. Their success does not depend on the rationality of their programs, because they are all equally swayed by wishful thinking. Rather, it depends on whether their clock happens to show the right time. Sometimes it is clear to everyone outside the hard core of ideologically committed individuals that one program is better suited than another to the needs of the moment. At other times dissatisfaction with the current

18 It is sometimes said that in politics disagreement is rarely about values but usually about facts. This observation, though often correct, must be supplemented by pointing out that the explanation of factual disagreement is frequently to be found in value differences. The "cold" *content* of the beliefs over which people disagree then goes together with "hot" mechanisms for belief formation.

government is what determines whether the "time has come" for a new party.

A political ideology, to be successful, has to be couched in terms of the general interest. Marx argued, however, that success could be self-defeating. The French bourgeoisie, when successfully demanding the abolition of privileges, also prepared the ground for its own future defeat by admitting its future enemy to the political arena. The bourgeoisie would no doubt have liked an abolition of privileges tailor-made to its interests, but, as Tocqueville noticed, it is difficult to contain democracy once it has been introduced. When the idea of natural privileges ceased to be viable, the only remaining options were dictatorship, enforcing man-made privileges, and democracy, abolishing all privileges. Before the modern age, political ideology was still particularistic, presenting, in Marx's words, an almost zoological picture of the natural rights, duties, and obligations of the different social classes. When choosing to attack the very notion of natural privilege, rather than substituting one set of privilege holders for another, the bourgeoisie played the sorcerer's apprentice. The universalistic political ideology they created turned out to have consequences beyond what they had intended.

## ECONOMIC THOUGHT AS IDEOLOGY

Any reader of Marx's major economic writings will have been struck by the way he discusses the views of his opponents. Only occasionally does he follow the normal scholarly practice of arguing the merits of their case. Much more frequently he takes a reductionist approach, in which the views of other writers do not so much represent alternative approaches to the same economic reality as part of the reality to be explained. Occasionally this practice degenerates into *ad hominem* abuse, but it is not inherently objectionable. It can be justified both as a contribution to the sociology of knowledge and, less obviously, as part of economic analysis proper. The latter role arises because many of the economic theories that Marx dissects are, in his view, little more than systematic expressions of spontaneously arising economic illusions. To the extent that the economic agents themselves make their decisions on the basis of such illusionary beliefs, they have consequences for the production and distribution of goods.

Marx's critique of economic theory is stated at (needlessly) great length in the three volumes of *Theories of Surplus-Value*. These contain discussions of mercantilist and physiocratic doctrines, as well as extensive treatments of Adam Smith, Ricardo, Malthus, and a group of writers that Marx refers to as "vulgar economists." The two criticisms most frequently deployed are, first, that the economists do not go beyond the appearance of things to their real essence and, second, that their theories tend to serve as apologies for the existing capitalist system (or, in the case of the physiocrats, pave the way for its emergence).

Most economists are unable to go beyond the appearance of things to their inner essence. In their writings they do little more than restate the manner in which economic relations appear to the economic agents themselves, without any attempt to penetrate more deeply into the nature of things. "But all science would be superfluous if the outward appearance and the essence of things directly coincided." In the 1861–3 *Critique* Marx compares his critique of political economy to the Copernican revolution, which similarly amounted to a denial of the apparent movement of the sun around the earth. Only in communism will social relations become perfectly transparent and the essence immediately coincide with the appearance, which also means that the need for a social science will disappear.

The essence–appearance distinction, as applied by Marx, is ambiguous because the appearance, that which appears, allows for two different antonyms. It may be contrasted with what is hidden, and accessible only by the mediation of thought. In this sense one might say, for example, that behind the visual appearance of a table is the atomic structure that forms its essence. This was how Marx conceived the relation between prices and labor values. The latter are hidden magnitudes that are not subjective realities for the economic agents, who make their decisions in terms of the observable prices. Yet, he argued, in order to explain prices it is necessary to go behind the veil of appearance and determine the values. The argument is invalid, because equilibrium prices can be determined without any reference to labor values.[19]

Another reading of the distinction is inherently more interesting. Here the salient feature of the appearance is that it is *local* – what appears always appears to a person occupying a particular standpoint and observing the phenomena from a particular perspective. Any given appearance may be contrasted with the *global network* of appearances, which is not tied to any particular standpoint. An example is the distinction between partial equilibrium and general equilibrium in economics. In partial equilibrium analysis we consider an agent who is confronting a decision problem in which the behavior of other firms is taken for given. In reality, of course, the behavior of other firms is not "given" to them but represents solutions to *their* decision problems. A full understanding of the situation requires simultaneous consideration of all these decision problems, as in general equilibrium analysis. A general equilibrium must be a partial equilibrium for each economic agent.

Examples abound in Marx's writing of the distinction between local appearance and global essence. Their general purpose is to show how, in an unplanned economy, the isolation of the economic agents from each other distorts their understanding of the economic relations that obtain among them. (In addition, but only partly because of lack of insight, this isolation tends to produce bad outcomes.) Locally speaking, any agent can make a profit from buying cheap and selling dear. Globally speaking, this is impossible: A system of circular cheating is logically impossible. Yet, Marx observed, some writers committed the fallacy of arguing that general profits could arise in circulation, wrongly believing that what was possible for *any* commodity owner taken separately was possible for *all* of them taken simultaneously. Similarly, it is locally true of each capital owner that he has a choice between investing his capital in a productive enterprise and depositing it in a bank in

19 Actually, Marx was guilty of the very fallacy – the confusion of essence and appearance – that he imputed to his opponents. His procedure for deriving prices from values involved using the rate of profit as a markup on labor values, thereby committing the dialectical howler of admitting values to the realm of appearance.

order to draw interest on it. Again, this is impossible on a global scale, because if all capitalists decided to become rentiers none of them would get an interest on his capital.[20] Yet, Marx argued, the vulgar economists actually believe that interest-bearing capital has a life of its own, independent of the productive activities that alone can support it. The mercantilists were especially prone to such fallacies. A quite different kind of example arises with respect to the relation between labor and capital. Because capitalism, unlike earlier modes of production, allows the worker the freedom to choose his own master, it may appear as if labor is more independent of capital than is actually the case. Although there is no capitalist for whom the worker has to work, he has to work for some capitalist or other. The freedom of choice obscures the structural dependency.

The other main criticism Marx addresses to the bourgeois economists is that their goal is not to reach a correct understanding of the capitalist economy but to provide apologies for it. The closest approximation to a truly scientific approach is that of Adam Smith and Ricardo who, for instance, were willing to draw the logical conclusion that the landowners were a parasitic class with no useful economic function. Malthus, writing in the cynical tradition of Bernard Mandeville's "private vices, public benefits," argued that an idle class of landowners and other unproductive agents was necessary to ensure that there was sufficient demand for the goods produced. The "vulgar economists" – Senior, Bastiat, Carey, and others – used a somewhat different argument when they referred to land, capital, and labor as factors of production, all of which performed useful productive functions entitling their owners to a reward. Again, however, the effect of their work was apologetic. In Raymond Aron's phrase, they offered a "sociodicy," a secular version of the theodicy: an argument that the existing society is the best of all possible societies and that all apparent blemishes have an indispensable function for the whole.

The second line of argument is much less interesting than the first. Marx writes as if a doctrine could be refuted by the mere

---

20 Conversely, if all capitalists simultaneously decided to withdraw their money from the bank, it would go bankrupt and nobody would get his money.

demonstration that it serves group or class interests. Because virtually any theory is likely to fit the interest of some group, this argument is too strong: If accepted, it would leave no survivors. Generally speaking, when the ideological character of a doctrine is shown by its *acceptation* by a specific class, the demonstration has no implications for its truth or falsity. By contrast, when one can show that a certain view is contaminated at the level of *production*, there is a strong presumption against its being true. A doctrine that is accepted for social reasons does not lose any claim to being true; a doctrine whose emergence in the first place is due to irrelevant social reasons – class interest or class position – is unlikely to be correct, except by accident.

Marx's treatment of the physiocrats deserves special mention because of its frankly teleological perspective. Marx correctly points to a paradoxical feature of their doctrine, that under the guise of glorifying landed property they actually promoted industrial capitalism. The physiocrats claimed that only land was really productive and that industry was essentially "sterile." Again, their view stemmed from excessive reliance on the appearance of things. Because surplus creation in agriculture occurs in a much more tangible form than in industry, they were led to deny that it ever takes place in the latter. Yet from this misguided view they drew a consequence that was very favorable to industrial interests, namely, that industry, being sterile, ought to be exempt from taxation. Marx then takes the further step of arguing, or strongly suggesting, that this historical irony actually explains the emergence of the physiocrat doctrine. Not content with pointing out the paradox, he had to assign it a meaning or function in his wider historical scheme – that of preparing the ground for capitalism from within the womb of precapitalist society.

## RELIGION AS IDEOLOGY

Among the Young Hegelians, critique of religion was a constant preoccupation. Marx was especially influenced by Feuerbach's view that religion is a form of projection of the human essence onto a divine being, who is then invested with power over man. In religion man creates God, who appears to man as his creator. This conception of an inversion of subject and object, of creator and created, is at the origin of Marx's concept of alienation. Man becomes the slave of his own products in economic life by the subsumption of labor under capital; in politics, by the usurpation of power by representatives or delegates; and in religion, by the subjection of man to an imaginary divine being. Marx believed that in communism all these forms of alienation would disappear: There would no social or psychological inertia by which the results of human action or the products of the human mind could take on an independent existence. Economic self-enslavement will disappear when the collective producers take possession of the means of production. Political alienation will be eliminated first by making all representatives instantly revocable (under the dictatorship of the proletariat), and then by the society becoming so transparent that the need for politics itself withers away. Religion, finally, will disappear together with the conditions that made it necessary: misery, class rule, commodity production.

Marx never offered a sustained analysis of religion. As is frequently the case, we have to extract his views from a number of brief passages scattered in various writings. To impose some structure on them, we may employ a distinction between the *fact* of religion and the specific *content*. All class societies have had some form of religion: This fact in itself demands an explanation. Next, we would like to be able to explain why different societies have had different religious systems: why some have been monotheistic, others not; why some societies espouse Catholicism, others Protestantism, and so on. It would appear that Marx proposes a hot, or motivational, explanation of the general fact of religion, and a cold, or cognitive, analysis of the varying content. All class societies have religion, because religion serves certain important interests linked to class subjection and class domination. Capitalism has Christianity because of cognitive affinities between the two systems.

The interest-related explanation of religion is twofold. In the early article, "Contribution to the critique of Hegel's Philosophy of Law: Introduction," religion is characterized, along Feuerbachian lines, as "the general theory of [the social] world, its encyclopaedic compendium, its logic in popular form, its spiritualistic *point*

*d'honneur,* its enthusiasm, its moral sanction, its solemn comple-
ment, its universal source of consolation and justification. . . . Religion is the sigh of the oppressed creature, the heart of a heartless
world, just as it is the spirit of spiritless conditions. It is the *opium* of
the people." The analytical core of this exuberant rhetoric seems
to be that religion arises spontaneously within the mind, as a
form of dissonance reduction: "the sigh of the oppressed creature."[21] A few years later he offered a more "Marxist" (or proto-
Nietzschean) account, to the effect that religion encourages "cow-
ardice, self-contempt, abasement, submissiveness and humble-
ness" and thereby prevents the oppressed from revolting against
their state. Here the argument seems to be that religion is to be
explained by how it serves the interests of the ruling class, not by
the fulfillment of a need of the exploited classes.

E. P. Thompson's study of working-class Methodism in the Industrial Revolution offers a more nuanced picture. He shows how
religion, though inculcated by the industrial capitalists, also met
autonomous needs of the workers. Moreover, the inculcation was
in no way a cynical manipulation. The faith of the employers was
as strong and genuine as that of the workers; indeed, as Paul
Veyne argues in a different context, it had to be if the inculcation
was to be successful. It would be wildly implausible to argue that
the religious belief of the employers could be explained by this
fact, that is, by the need to have a genuine faith in order to be able
to persuade the workers to adopt religious beliefs that work out to
the benefit of the employers. Although it may be possible to adopt
religious beliefs at will, motivated by the extrinsic benefits of having the belief rather than by intrinsic faith, the intellectual contor-
tions necessary for this feat disqualify it as an explanation of mass
religion. Another alternative – an unsupported functional explanation – is no better, and a well-supported functional explanation
has not been forthcoming.

Why, then, would employers have religious beliefs? More generally, what is the connection between religion and capitalism?
This problem, made famous by Max Weber, also preoccupied

21 Although this passage was written two years before the formulation of historical materialism, it cannot be dismissed as a youthful "humanist aberration"
   because Marx makes essentially the same point in a manuscript from 1865.

Marx. Weber's question was: Did Calvinism predispose to specifically capitalist behavior, such as a high rate of savings and investment? His affirmative answer relied on a hot psychological mechanism. According to Calvin's doctrine of predestination, there was nothing the entrepreneurs could do to achieve salvation, but by engaging in "inner-worldly asceticism" they could and did achieve the certainty of being among the elect. E. P. Thompson asks a different question: Did capitalist activities predispose toward Puritanism? His affirmative answer again relies on a motivational mechanism. Puritanism contributed to "the psychic energy and social coherence of middle-class groups" – an argument that in the absence of further details looks like an unsupported functional explanation.

Marx also asked Thompson's question, or one very much like it, and like him offered an affirmative answer. The nature of the answer is, however, entirely different, because Marx relies exclusively on various cold, cognitive connections. Unfortunately, these are implausible taken separately and inconsistent taken jointly. In his comments on the links among capitalism, Protestantism, and Catholicism Marx set a disastrous precedent for many later writers who have attempted to find "structural homologies" or "isomorphisms" (two fancy terms for "similarities") between economic structures and mental products. Because virtually any two entities can be said to resemble each other in some respect,[22] this practice has no other constraints than the inventiveness and ingenuity of the writer: There are no reality constraints and no reality control.

Marx suggests two inconsistent lines of argument. One is that there is a strong connection between mercantilism and Protestantism, the other that there is an elective affinity between mercantilism and Catholicism. He was confused, apparently, by the fact that money has two distinct features that point to different religious modes. On the one hand, money (gold and silver), unlike credit, can be hoarded. Hoarding easily turns into an obsession, which is related to the fanatical self-denying practices of extreme

---

22 Cf. the following "law of family likenesses": For any two members of a family there exists a third who asserts that there is a strong resemblance between them.

Protestantism. On the other hand, money can be seen as the "incarnation" or "transubstantiation" of real wealth. In that sense the monetary fetishism associated with mercantilism is related to the specifically Catholic practice of investing relics and the like with supernatural significance. Both arguments are asserted several times by Marx, each serving to show up the essential arbitrariness of the other. Later attempts to explain the theology of Port Royal, the philosophy of Descartes, or the physics of Newton in terms of similarities with the underlying economic structure are equally arbitrary. Like the analogies between societies and organisms that flourished around the turn of the century, they belong to the cabinet of horrors of scientific thought. Their common ancestor is the theory of "signs" that flourished in the century prior to the scientific revolution inaugurated by Galileo – the idea that there are natural, noncausal correspondences between different parts of the universe. What Keith Thomas refers to as the "short-lived union of science and magic" maintained a subterranean existence of which the doctrine of ideology, in one of its versions, has been one manifestation.

## BIBLIOGRAPHY

*Introduction.* There are many books that contain discussions of Marx's theory of ideology. The only ones that can be fully recommended are Raymond Geuss, *The Idea of a Critical Theory* (Cambridge University Press, 1981), and chapter 5 of G. A. Cohen's *Karl Marx's Theory of History* (Oxford University Press, 1978). There are also many books that discuss the relation between Marx and Freud; to my knowledge, none of them can be recommended. For valuable discussions of cold cognitive mechanisms, see D. Kahneman, P. Slovic and A. Tversky (eds.), *Judgment under Uncertainty* (Cambridge University Press, 1982), and R. Nisbett and L. Ross, *Human Inference: Strategies and Shortcomings of Social Judgment* (Prentice-Hall, 1981). Good accounts of hot cognitive distortions include L. Festinger, *A Theory of Cognitive Dissonance* (Stanford University Press, 1957), and D. Pears, *Motivated Irrationality* (Oxford University Press, 1984). A good introduction to (non-Marxist) sociology of knowledge is in Robert Merton's *Social Theory and Social Structure* (Free Press, 1968).

*Political ideologies.* Alexis de Tocqueville's *Democracy in America* (Anchor Books, 1969) and the notebooks from his American journey, *Voyages en*

*Sicile et aux Etats-Unis* (Gallimard, 1957), anticipate many of Marx's views and remain passionately interesting. A useful account of ideological struggles during the French revolution is P. Higonnet, *Class, Ideology, and the Rights of Nobles during the French Revolution* (Oxford University Press, 1981). Paul Veyne, *Le Pain et le Cirque* (Editions du Seuil, 1976), is an immensely stimulating application of Festinger's work to political ideologies in classical antiquity.

*Economic thought as ideology*. For the idea of a withering away of social science in communism, see Cohen, *Marx's Theory of History*, app. 2. For the local-global fallacy, see my *Logic and Society* (Wiley, 1978), chap. 5.

*Religion as ideology*. A good introduction to Feuerbach's thought is M. Wartofsky, *Feuerbach* (Cambridge University Press, 1977). Max Weber's views on religion and capitalism are set out in *The Protestant Ethic and the Spirit of Capitalism* (Scribner, 1958). E. P. Thompson's argument is found in chapter 14 of *The Making of the English Working Class* (Penguin, 1968). For the problem of believing at will, see my *Ulysses and the Sirens* (Cambridge University Press, 1979), chap. 2, sec. 3. Marxist treatments of Port Royal, Descartes, and Newton are found in, respectively, L. Goldmann, *Le Dieu Caché* (Gallimard, 1954); F. Borkenau, *Die Übergang vom feudalen zum bürgerlichen Weltbild* (Alcan, 1934); and B. Hessen, "The social and economic roots of Newton's *Principia*," in N. Bukharin (ed.), *Science at the Cross Roads* (Kniga, 1931), pp. 147–212. The theory and practice of signs is discussed in K. Thomas, *Religion and the Decline of Magic* (Penguin, 1973).

# 10

# WHAT IS LIVING AND WHAT IS DEAD IN THE PHILOSOPHY OF MARX?

## INTRODUCTION

THE title of this chapter is adapted from Benedetto Croce's book, *What Is Living and What Is Dead in the Philosophy of Hegel?* There is little new in it, compared to the preceding chapters. Its task is to dot the *i*'s and cross the *t*'s, so as to provide the reader with a convenient summary. In order to avoid ending on an anticlimactic note, I reverse the order of the title. I first consider the elements of Marx's thought that in my opinion are dead, including some that are artificially kept alive and ought to be buried. I conclude by discussing elements that I consider to be alive, including some that are widely believed to be dead and hence in need of resurrection.

There are several grounds on which one can argue a theory to be dead. First, it may be inapplicable today, even though correct when first stated. Because society changes, statements that were true a hundred years ago may be false today. Second, the theory may have been false even when originally formulated, although by no fault of its author. If his theory was the best that could be stated given the data or the analytical techniques available at the time, one should not blame him if it is superseded in the light of later developments. Third, the theory may have been false at the time of inception, in the light of the available data and techniques. A special case is when the theory can be shown to be false on purely logical grounds, prior to the inspection of data. In the evaluation of Marx's theories carried out here, all of these criteria are invoked. Sometimes more than one of them applies to a given theory. It would be pointlessly pedantic to spell out in each particular case what criteria are being used in what combination, but the reader should keep the distinction in mind.

To illustrate the distinction, consider three cases. It can be argued that mid-nineteenth-century Europe was historically unique in several respects. It realized the pure concept of property, as full and exclusive *jus uti et abuti*, whereas at all earlier and later times the property of a thing has been conceived as a bundle of rights (and obligations) that could be and usually was split among several persons. It allowed for a maximum of separation between the economic and the political spheres, as a distinction among different sets of people, whereas in earlier and later societies the distinction has been one among roles or even aspects of roles. It brought class struggle to the forefront as the main determinant of social conflict, whereas at earlier and later times issues of cultural identity – race, nation, gender, language, religion – have been no less important. It approximated to a high degree the pure model of a competitive market economy, whereas in earlier and later modes of production cartels, monopolies, and state intervention have been much more prominent. These statements, which I believe to be at least roughly true, suggest that Marx sometimes erred because he did not recognize what an exceptional society he was observing. Much of what he said may have been approximately true at the time, but the backward and forward extensions were frequently less successful.

Next, consider Marx as an economic historian. We know today that his views on the Asiatic mode of production, shared by many of his contemporaries, rested on inadequate information, although probably the best available at the time. We are in a much better position than he was to assess technological change during the Middle Ages, and as a result we can discard his views that essentially no innovation occurred from late antiquity until the modern age. We know that his views about the relation between the eighteenth-century British enclosures and the supply of labor to industry, though shared by all economic historians until recently, are in fact false. The enclosures, far from being labor-saving, were labor-using; the industrial work force grew out of a general population increase. We can hardly blame Marx for not considering monopoly behavior as a possible explanation of the employers' interest in a reduction of the working day, because the analytical tools for the study of monopoly did not exist at his time. All of these are examples of what, in the above classification, corresponds to the second kind of mistakes: Marx was wrong, but it is hard to see how he could have done much better.

The third kind of mistakes are the most disturbing, in that they reflect upon the quality of Marx's judgment. There is some dishonesty in his handling of empirical evidence, as when Marx updates British economic statistics when it suits him but retains the older figures when they support his case. Certainly there is no trace in his writings of the scholarly practice known as playing the devil's advocate. There are strong elements of wishful thinking, which, if morally less deplorable than dishonesty, probably had a more destructive impact on the quality of his work. Moreover, there are many examples of prejudice, as in his attitude toward Napoleon III or Lord Palmerston. Finally, his economic theories abound with purely logical mistakes. The labor theory of value and the theory of the falling rate of profit are very poor specimens of deductive reasoning.

Against all this, we need to remind ourselves that although Marx's passion often clouded his judgment it also sustained his sometimes superhuman efforts and his genuinely great achievements. On the one hand, motivation and good judgment both contribute to success; on the other hand, motivation easily subverts judgment. To wish for the first effect of motivation without the second may be to ask for the impossible. Beliefs born of passion serve passion badly, but if lack of passion is a condition for impartial judgment, as some recent psychological findings suggest, the price may be higher than we want to pay.

### WHAT IS DEAD?

1. Scientific socialism is dead. There is no way in which a political theory can dispense with values and rely instead on the laws of history operating with iron necessity. There exists no intellectually respectable argument for the view that history is subject to a progressive pattern that can be detected in the past and extrapolated into the future. To disprove this view, it is sufficient to point to the possibility of a nuclear war, leading to the extinction of mankind.

How could historical materialism offer an a priori refutation of this possibility? Moreover, there is no reason to expect history to have the property of *homeorhesis*, or dynamic stability. Think of a ball rolling down the bottom of a valley. The process is dynamically stable, because if the ball is pushed off course and sent up the hillside it will sooner or later return to the bottom again – unless the push is a very strong one, so that the ball is sent over into the adjoining valley. A nuclear war would certainly be a very strong push. Without dynamic stability, however, even small pushes could change the course of history.

A special case is "the role of the individual in history." Any deterministic macrohistorical theory must deny that the actions of a single individual can influence history in a significant way, but denial is not enough; an argument is also required. None has been forthcoming. Tolstoy's mathematical analogy in *War and Peace*, that individuals are like infinitesimally small magnitudes whose actions are aggregated into history by a process akin to mathematical integration, is very much in the spirit of scientific socialism. It is also very misleading, because social interaction is not an additive process. The action of one individual can make a small or a large difference to the outcome, depending on his place in the network of social relations.

Scientific socialism is also flawed in its treatment of values. The horns of the dilemma are well known. Either the laws of history operate with such iron necessity that political action is superfluous – communism will somehow come about "by itself" without propaganda, leadership, or mass action – or, if this view is discarded, as it must be, political action must be guided by values. One might think that communism, though ultimately inevitable, is also undesirable and therefore try to stave it off for as long as possible. If one thinks communism is desirable, value problems may also arise. To say, with Marx, that the role of action is to "shorten and lessen the birth pangs" is to beg the question, for what if the choice is between a short, violent delivery and a long, more peaceful one? In that case, what are the principles that allow one to choose between different courses of action? Are they purely utilitarian ones, or are they to some extent also constrained by individual rights? Uncertainty and moral responsibility are part and parcel of political action. To deny that they are testifies to intellectual hubris and moral blindness.

2. Dialectical materialism is dead. This doctrine, like scientific socialism, is mainly associated with Engels, but it is also a minor strand in Marx's thought. In the first place, there is no coherent and interesting sense in which any of the central views in Marxism are "materialist." No Marxist philosopher has offered any useful insights on the problems of philosophical materialism, such as the mind–body problem, the sense–data problem, and the like. And even if Marxism had a specific, well-defined, and well-defended version of philosophical materialism, it would bear no interesting relation to historical materialism. In vague and general terms, both doctrines can be summarized in the statement, "Being determines consciousness." As soon, however, as one attempts to make the statement more precise, the similarity disappears. According to historical materialism, ideas are both separate from and capable of having a causal impact on the economic structure; no similar statement would hold for any form of philosophical materialism.

In the second place, the form of dialectics codified in dialectical materialism is quite trivial. Sometimes it amounts to little more than a statement of the general interconnections among all things, and at other times it is used as a fancy phrase for feedback processes. The "laws of dialectics" stated by Engels are somewhat less vacuous, although far from laws in the ordinary sense of the term. They can serve as useful reminders that some natural and historical processes are irreversible, nonlinear, and even discontinuous. "Mechanical materialism," a phrase used as the antonym of dialectical materialism, might then be defined as the view (or implicit assumption) that all processes are reversible and linear, except that the term "materialism" does not serve any useful purpose here.

3. Teleology and functionalism are dead. In Marx's thought, a teleological philosophy of history became wedded, in an apparently paradoxical way, to scientific socialism. The paradox is that teleology explains everything by backward connections, from the end to be realized to the means that realize it, whereas science proceeds by forward connections from cause to effect. In the the-

ological tradition that forms the backdrop to Marx's thinking, the paradox is readily acknowledged. As Leibniz wrote, "There are two realms, that of efficient causes and that of final causes, and each is sufficient to explain everything in detail, as if the other did not exist." When God created the universe, he set up the causal chain that would best realize his goal, so that each link in the chain can be explained both as the effect of its predecessor in the chain and as being part of an optimal chain.

This reconciliation of teleology and causality presupposes theological premises and, in particular, the existence of a divine subject. For Leibniz, history had a goal and a creator. These two, of course, go together. Hegel has been praised for seeing that history is a process without a subject. Yet he also retained, disastrously, the idea that history has a goal, as if the concept of a goal had a meaning apart from a subject for whom it is a goal. This Hegelian vision retained a strong grip on Marx's thinking, at least in many of his writings. The main exception is *The German Ideology,* which espouses a robustly antiteleological view. In the major economic writings, he reverted to the Hegelianism of his early youth, arguing that the immanent purpose of history was to carry mankind through the Purgatory of alienation and class conflict toward communism, because full unity could not be achieved in any other way than by a temporary loss of unity. This is individual rationality writ large, as if Humanity were a supraindividual actor with the capacity to defer gratification.

Another supraindividual entity mysteriously endowed with powers to act is Capital. The numerous instances of functional explanation in Marx's writings usually take the form of arguing that some institution or behavioral pattern works to the benefit of capital and then simply assuming that these benefits provide a sufficient explanation for its presence. Examples include the explanations of social mobility, physiocrat doctrines, labor-saving technical change, state power, the British Ten Hours Bill, and the prevalence of crime under capitalism. (The last-mentioned account, in *Theories of Surplus-Value,* is offered as a parody of Mandeville's "private vices, public benefits" and is not in itself evidence for a tendency to rely on unsupported functional explanation. Yet later Marxist criminologists have taken it seriously and written about the benefits of crime against property to the property-owning class.)

The point is not that these accounts are necessarily false but that Marx does not provide us with any reasons for thinking that they are true. There exist forms of functional explanation that do not rely simply on the presence of benefits but either specify a mechanism by which the benefits maintain their causes or provide lawlike statements that, even in the absence of knowledge of the mechanism, could be used to back the explanation. Marx and most of his followers have not, unfortunately, felt any need or obligation to justify their use of functional explanation.

4. Marxian economic theory is dead, with one important exception: the theory of technical change. (This exception is discussed in the section "What Is Living?") The labor theory of value is intellectually bankrupt. The very concept of the labor content of a commodity is ill defined in the presence of heterogeneous labor or heterogeneous work tasks. Even assuming that the concept could be defined, it has no useful role to perform. The equilibrium prices and rate of profit can be determined without invoking labor values. If any connection obtains, it is rather the other way around: Prices must be known before we can deduce labor values. The labor theory of value does not provide a useful criterion for the choice of socially desirable techniques, nor does it explain the actual choice of technique under capitalism. It vitiates the otherwise important theory of fetishism and detracts from the otherwise effective criticism of vulgar economy. Nor does the labor theory of value offer any useful insights into the possibility of stable exchange rates and of surplus.

The other main pillar of Marxian economic theory, the theory that the rate of profit tends to fall as a result of labor-saving technical change, is equally untenable. Although superficially attractive because of its pleasingly "dialectical" appearance, it turns out to have a number of fatal flaws. Most importantly, Marx neglected the fact that even labor-saving technical change has the indirect effect of depreciating the value of constant capital, thereby counteracting and possibly offsetting the tendency of the rate of profit to fall. Moreover, Marx offers no argument for the view that technical change tends to be labor-saving. The other crisis theories sketched by Marx are even less convincing, because they are not even stated with sufficient precision to allow for evaluation or refutation. The theory of the falling rate of profit passes this test: It is falsifiable, and indeed false, contrary not just to intuition but to truth as well.

5. The theory of productive forces and relations of production – perhaps the most important part of historical materialism – is dead. This obituary may be more controversial than the others; there is probably more room here for reasonable doubt. The main objection to the view that property relations rise and fall according to their tendency to promote or hinder the development of the productive forces is that it has no microfoundations. Marx does not explain how the tendency is translated into a social force, sustained by the motivations of individual men. Moreover, the view is inherently less plausible than an alternative account, according to which property relations are determined by their tendency to promote or hinder surplus maximization. Individuals have a motive to maximize surplus; only Humanity, in its striving toward communism, has a motive to maximize the rate of innovation.

In addition to being unsupported and implausible, Marx's doctrine is inconsistent with what he actually writes about the various historical modes of production. As he describes it, the transition from slavery to feudalism did not go together with an increase in the rate of innovation. His account of the transition from feudalism to capitalism relies more on surplus maximization than on innovation. His predictions for the transition to communism invoke the suboptimal use of techniques under capitalism rather than their suboptimal rate of change. One might almost say that the obituary for the general theory, as stated in the 1859 preface to *A Critique of Political Economy*, has already been written by Marx himself, for he consistently refuses to adopt it in his own historical studies.

6. Other parts of Marx's theory can be declared neither unambiguously dead nor unambiguously well and alive. The theories of alienation, exploitation, class, politics, and ideology are to some extent vitiated by wishful thinking, functional explanation, and

sheer arbitrariness, but they also offer vital, even crucial insights. Rather than discussing under separate headings what is dead and what is alive, I consider these aspects together below.

1. The dialectical method, or at least one version of it, is certainly alive. Not everything Marx learned from Hegel led him astray. Although Hegel's *Logic* is among the most obscure books ever written, *The Phenomenology of Spirit* is vastly more valuable, which is not to say that it is easy reading. Marx was under the influence of both. Sometimes he seems to espouse the doctrine of the *Logic,* that the world is contradictory in the sense that two mutually inconsistent statements can both be true. This view, frankly, is nonsense. Other analyses seem to draw on the *Phenomenology,* which offered an account of real contradictions that does not commit one to this absurd view. What Marx refers to as social contradictions correspond both to a certain type of logical fallacy ("the fallacy of composition") and to the perverse mechanisms whereby individually rational behavior generates collectively disastrous outcomes. Before Keynes, he diagnosed an essential paradox of capitalism in the fact that each employer wants his workers to have low wages and those employed by all other capitalists to have high wages. The theory of the falling rate of profit, though mathematically unsound, rests on a structurally similar mechanism. Against Adam Smith's view that the self-interest of the individual and the collective interest of society need not conflict but that, on the contrary, the latter can often be realized only through the former, Marx was more impressed by negative unintended consequences and by the self-defeating rationality of the Prisoner's Dilemma.

2. The theory of alienation is living, as is, correlatively, Marx's conception of the good life for man. By emphasizing the ideal of the self-realization of the individual, Marx wanted to mark his distance from two rival conceptions. First, the emphasis on the self-realization of the *individual* excludes any conception that places the self-realization of mankind at the center. Although Marx's commitment to methodological individualism was intermittent at best, his eth-

ical individualism was unwavering. He hailed the contributions to science and culture made by class societies in general and by capitalism in particular, but he also recognized that they were achieved at the expense of lack of self-realization for the vast majority. Second, the emphasis on the *self-realization* of the individual excludes any conception of the good life as one of passive consumption, however enjoyable. His was an Aristotelian conception of the good life for man, as one in which men bring to reality their "species powers," that is, their creative potentialities. He did not ask or answer the question of why men ought to develop their species powers, but some responses can be suggested. Because of the economies of scale involved in self-realization, it is inherently more satisfactory than consumption. Also, self-realization allows the development of self-respect, without which even consumption loses most of its attractions. Finally, to the extent that self-realization leads to more people engaging in creative activities, others will benefit from what they create.

If properly modified and restricted, Marx's theory of self-realization is a good guide to industrial reform and, more ambitiously, to large-scale social and economic change. Some of the modifications are the following. It will not turn out to be possible for everybody to develop all their abilities, if only because this would prevent exploitation of the economies of scale. Nor can one expect that everyone will be able to find satisfaction in a restricted form of self-realization. Because it is difficult to know what one's abilities will turn out to be, there is always the risk that one may embark upon a mode of self-realization that is either too easy or too difficult, leading to boredom or frustration. Moreover, self-realization is demanding in that it requires some delay of gratification; not everyone might be willing to wait, especially as there is some uncertainty as to whether the result will be worth the sacrifice. Finally, it is uncertain to what extent complex industrial societies can be reorganized so as to allow universal scope for self-realization.

3. The theory of exploitation is living, as is, correlatively, Marx's conception of distributive justice. Although exploitation is not a fundamental moral concept, as it would be if exploiting someone ipso facto was doing something morally wrong, the theory provides a robust guide to what is right and wrong in a large number

of standard cases. These arise when people perform more labor than is needed to produce the goods they consume, for any of the following reasons: physical coercion, as in slavery and feudalism; economic coercion, as when employers interfere with alternative employment opportunities for workers; or economic necessity, as when people, by no fault of their own, are forced to sell their labor power. The underlying principle of distributive justice is "To each according to his contribution," deviations from which can be justified only on grounds of special needs. Neither the contribution principle nor the principle whereby needs justify deviations from it is clearly stated by Marx, although, again, they can serve as useful first approximations.

To see why exploitation is not a fundamental moral concept, consider two cases. Imagine first that current injustices have been eliminated and that society can start from a clean slate, whatever that means. (What it means would depend on which finer approximation to distributive justice one adopts.) If under these conditions some people save more than others, who prefer immediate consumption over delayed consumption, and if the former offer jobs to the latter that would involve exploiting them, on what grounds could anyone object to such "capitalistic acts among consenting adults"? It would seem perverse to punish practices that do not impose harm on anybody and that are the result of freely undertaken, mutually beneficial contracts. Although some of the arguments developed with respect to other "victimless crimes," such as gambling or prostitution, might sometimes apply here, one can also think of circumstances in which they would not be relevant. Second, imagine that the persons who own most of the capital also have a very strong preference for consumption over leisure, in which case one can construct cases in which the rich will offer themselves out for hire to the poor, who do not want to use even what little capital they have. Although strictly speaking the poor would then exploit the rich, they would not be doing anything morally wrong. Exploitation, when wrong, is wrong not just because it is exploitation but because of some further features. Hence, the concept of exploitation has mainly a descriptive and heuristic function, which, in any actual inquiry into social injustice, can be a very important one.

4. Marx's theory of technical change is definitely living. Some of the most exciting chapters of *Capital I* are those in which Marx dissects the relations among technology, profit, power, and property rights at the level of the firm. When the capitalist confronts his workers, he does not simply deal with a "factor of production" that is to be combined optimally with other factors of production. The workers have a capacity for individual and collective resistance, which can be affected by the specific organization of the work process, including the choice of technology. Because their capacity for resistance affects the wage the capitalist has to pay the workers, the effective cost of employing them is partly decided within the firm, not only by outside market conditions. Hence, the employer may have an incentive not to introduce new technology if it goes together with a physical reorganization than enhances the solidarity or bargaining power of the workers or if it involves prohibitively high costs of supervision. (On the other hand – and this is an aspect that Marx did not stress – the workers may have an incentive to restrict their freedom of action, so that the capitalists will not be deterred from introducing new techniques that allow scope for improvement for both parties.) This problem may create a free-rider difficulty among the employers, if the solidarity-enhancing effect of new technology occurs only if it is widely adopted.

5. Marx's theory of class consciousness, class struggle, and politics is vibrantly alive, although it is generally recognized that it does not provide the full answer to the questions that motivate its construction. At the most general level, one would expect a theory of classes to provide some flesh and blood for the abstract theory of productive forces and relations of production. If this was Marx's intention, he failed to carry it out. The latter theory fails, as noted, precisely because Marx did not show how social classes and the individuals who make them up would want to link their fate with a new social arrangement just because it promises a higher rate of innovation.

At another level, Marx believed that his theory of class offered the key to the understanding of social conflict. He thought deeply about the conditions under which members of a class were likely to act in a concerted way, that is, to become collective actors in the arena of social conflict. He emphasized, among other things, spatial isolation, high turnover rates, and cultural heterogeneity as obstacles to class consciousness. He had, moreover, pioneering insights into the nature of class conflict, class cooperation, and class coalitions. Because members of different classes may have common interests and common enemies, one cannot take it for granted that the class struggle is one of implacable opposition, at least not in the short or medium term. Today we would emphasize more than Marx did that the class struggle is also blurred by the presence of other, cross-cutting conflicts. There is no doubt that class is one important source of social conflict in Northern Ireland, South Africa, or Poland, but one would have to be very dogmatic to assert that it is the only or the dominant element. Religious, racial, and nationalistic sentiments have proved to be independent focuses of loyalty and organization. Marxism is not really able to come to grips with this fact, except by the somewhat desperate measure of arguing that in the very long run, defined by the emergence of a new mode of production, these cultural struggles have little importance – a statement that seems both false and somewhat irrelevant.

Finally, Marx wanted the class theory to provide an explanation of political phenomena and in particular of the behavior of the state in capitalist societies. The theory for which he is best known, that the state is "nothing but" a tool for the collective class interests of the capitalists, is one that he himself abandoned early on, when it was disproved by the turn of events in the main European countries around 1850. Instead, he proposed an "abdication theory" of the state, according to which the state is allowed to have some autonomy but only because it suits the interests of the capitalists. A closer look at this theory, however, shows that the autonomy granted to the aristocratic-feudal-bureaucratic governments in England, Germany, and France was quite substantial. Indeed, it would not be a great exaggeration to say that in Marx's historical writings, as opposed to his more theoretical pronouncements, the autonomy of the modern state is a cornerstone. The reason why Marx did not fully acknowledge this fact must be sought partly in his reluctance to abandon his general theory of history, in which the derivative nature of the political superstructure was equally much of a cornerstone. In part it may also be found in his insufficient grasp of the strategic nature of politics and of the fact that a political system can assign power in ways that do not correspond to the prepolitical resources of the actors. These flaws should not, however, obscure Marx's insight that the state depends structurally on the capitalist class, simply because its self-interest compels it to take some account of the interest of that class. How much account it must take is a strictly empirical matter, which cannot be prejudged by appealing to the general statements of historical materialism.

6. The theory of ideology is not particularly well and alive, but I believe it can and should be resurrected. Of all Marxist doctrines, this more than any other has been brought into disrepute by the arbitrary procedures adopted. Sometimes functional explanation has been the culprit, sometimes the even less intersubjectively valid method of looking for "similarities" between economic and mental activities. The first step to remedy the situation must be to draw upon the rich insights of cognitive psychology and its accumulated evidence about the motivational and cognitive processes that distort belief formation and preference formation. In fact, there could potentially be a two-way influence. The Marxist tradition in the sociology of knowledge might be able to suggest some specific hypotheses that could be tested by rigorous experimental procedures. One might, for instance, try to specify in a testable way the idea that the economic agents' perception of economic causality depends on their location in the economic system. Similarly, some forms of hot ideology formation, such as the motivated preference for some economic theories rather than others, would not seem to be outside the reach of experimental research. These are proposals for the future. The immediate task is to achieve recognition for the fact that the theory of ideology must have microfoundations if it is to go beyond its present stage, which is partly anecdotal, partly functionalist, partly conspiratorial, and partly magical.

Above all, the sheer vitality of Marx's thinking makes it impossible to think of him as anything but alive. His endless curiosity, vast culture, burning commitment, and brilliant intellect combined to create a mind with whom we can still communicate across the century that has passed. Commitment, of course, is not a value in itself; commitment to the wrong goals can be disastrous. Marx's goals were generous and liberating: self-realization for the individual, equality among individuals. His utopian attitude and lack of intellectual control prevented him from carrying out the theoretical and practical tasks he had set for himself, but without these qualities he would not even have tried. He suffered the cost; we are the beneficiaries.